UNSTOPPABLE

A Survival Guide for Parents:
Special Education Services for an
IEP or 504 Plan

With God all things are Possible

Raja B. Marhaba

Raja B Marhaba

With God all
things are
possible

Defining Moments Press, Inc.

Cover Design: Defining Moments Press, Inc.

Editing: Amber Torres

UNSTOPPABLE

Book Reviews

"OMG Your writing is amazing. I was glued to the book. I read it all the way through in one sitting. Your voice is perfect. This is a must read! I seriously cannot find a single item to critique except that you had me glued to the pages and I wished it was longer.

My eyes teared up when I read what you wrote about me. I wish I had been in a position then to ensure that the entire staff knew about 504s, Universal Design Learning, and, most of all, compassion and empathy. Please know that your family's journey influenced my own professional practice, and I helped develop one of the most robust 504 support programs at my current schools. I have never forgotten!"

- Dr. Aviva Ebner
Educator

"Raja Marhaba's Story Unstoppable, was an enjoyable fast read for anyone who's familiar with the public schools systems in the United States, I myself am dyslexic, and the family's journey of challenges and triumphs resonated with my own experience. This story is a must read for any family with kids. From my experience I can say there's not a more complete easy to follow roadmap for families whose children have special needs."

- Seth Wiener
Serial Entrepreneur

"UNSTOPPABLE is an amazing book. It is the story of one family's journey through the education system. It is a story of triumph by a mother for her children over a bureaucracy while at the same time an indictment of that bureaucracy.

UNSTOPPABLE is well written and extremely thorough in sharing the odyssey of the Marhaba family. It also has much to provide to other families whose children have learning disabilities so that they may avoid many of the pitfalls that Raja Marhaba encountered in her family's journey.

The book is also very sobering. It is hard to believe in this day and age that families have to go through such travails to achieve what we all want - a decent education for our children."

- John F. Weitkamp
Attorney

"This book is a life-saving gift to parents who have a child with learning and other disabilities struggling through the twists and turns of how to survive and advocate for their child in the public school system. Get rid of some of the guilt, and use this as a guide that will save you years of figuring it out yourself. Raja has packed her 25 years of experience in this short read. Learn how to help expedite the IEP or 504 processes and your legal rights to get the services your child is entitled to under the law. Discover what could be happening behind the scenes at your public school.

Open the book and read page by page Raja's heart-wrenching experience with her own two sons and how she persevered and sacrificed much of her own life to fight for her boys all the way up to the 9th district federal court. She has fought for her boys and is now fighting for YOU! She has done the work, walked the walk, and dedicated her life to this work to help one child at a time. It is a labor of love sharing a blueprint guide in hopes of changing YOUR child's life. Time is ticking; you will see how long her own boys suffered as she tried to navigate the system. Thank you, Raja, for helping my own son from the time he was 12 years old; he is now 23 and making his way in life. He had what he needed to thrive because you taught me how to advocate for my child. This book is YOUR chance to do the same."

- Cathy Cimoch
Parent

"Unstoppable is an educational guide and story of perseverance, determination, and unconditional love. It provides invaluable insights and instructions in navigating our broken educational system, especially for kids with learning disabilities. This unfortunate, but inspiring journey shows the importance of family, friends, and true relationships. It also shows the result of standing-up for what you believe in and what is right, regardless of the ramifications. Finding the right experts and people advocating for you is imperative. But you also must be the master of your fate and the captain of your soul.

Raja Marhaba is a remarkable woman who is intelligent, tenacious, honest, caring and kind. She sacrificed everything and did whatever it took to fight to provide her boys the best opportunities she possible could. I admire her and what she accomplished.

I was fortunate to become very close with Omar Jr. professionally and personally. He just needed the right environment, opportunity, and people around him to blossom, which he did. I provided him opportunities and he made the best of them. He succeeded and will continue to do so. I am very proud of him. Jonathan also persevered and turned out to be a great person. He also is on his way to becoming a successful businessman. It is an honor and privilege to be good friends with them.

I served on the Jonathan Foundation's Board of Directors from it's beginning and for many years. It is a highly needed unique foundation that makes a huge difference in kids lives. Raja helped my nephew, which made a significant difference in his journey. I highly recommend reading and learning from this book, then take appropriate action!"

- Thomas Leffler
Serial Entrepreneur

"The Love and Concern for her two sons with learning disabilities turned a quiet and loving suburban wife and mother into a determined and laser focused crusader to never surrender to the "system" of injustice and abandonment of her sons by the Los Angeles Unified School District. Like a combat military officer, Raja set a plan and followed it to gain the support and proper education for her two sons by litigation at United States Supreme Court. One lady that today has never given up on challenging the political and educational system in Los Angeles. The tab has exceeded $????. Raja's unwavering love, compassion and courage to obtain justice for her sons turned into fierce advocacy for the voiceless. May God continue to push Raja's dedication to help other parents dealing with similar situations."

- Dennis P. Zine
Retired Law Enforcement Supervisor and Retired L.A. City Councilman

"Raja Marhaba has written and created a valuable must-have book for parents of children that have special needs, disabilities, or other challenges and need a complete guide navigating through the broken public school system. Her honesty and transparency of her own life experience with her two sons, Jonathan and Omar, drew me in, and I felt a deep personal connection from the beginning through the end. She has walked the walk through her own personal sacrifices, unyielding dedication, fierce studies, and preparation to be the advocate she is today. She goes through easy procedural steps in preparation for an IEP, gives a rich tool kit, and a breakdown of language and its meaning that will aid and enhance a parent's understanding of what they need to know as well as an abundance of resources. She breaks down the language well for parents such as Resources of Disability Rights education and basic special education acronyms and a glossary of terms. She walks you through what to expect at an IEP, a 504 Plan meeting, what mediation is, how valuable a parent's signature is, a variety of assessments, and all protocols of how to organize it all to fight for your children. She does this through her own life experiences and user-friendly steps for parents. This book is a one-of-a-kind treasure for parents. Raja has fought the good fight for many years, and she has laid it out for parents to learn from, to be a step ahead of a broken system so parents can be the best possible advocates for their children. Her super strength is her faith in God and love for children to receive the best possible education they can receive and reach their truest

potential. This book is full of incredible, inspirational, and heartfelt stories from Raja, and her two sons Jonathan and Omar. You will find stories from parents and students that she has advocated for that have each had their own challenges and how much they have grown and achieved by working with Raja. She offers continual support and makes you feel like you are sitting in the same room with her as she walks you through the process. I believe she has taken her treasured binder of all her tears, struggles, determination, experience, and knowledge and given parents everything they need to know while holding their hand through the entire process! As a parent of a child Raja has advocated for, I can truly attest to her ability to bring victory to a case that seemed to be impossible. She changed the course of our son's life as well as us as a family. Go get this book! – She wrote it for you!"

- Debra Hopkins
Founder and President of Breaking The Chains Foundation 501©3,
American Council on Exercise Health Coach and Behavior Change
Specialist

"Unstoppable is an incredible personal account of a family with two exceptional children forced into years of legal action to secure an appropriate education so their boys could learn to read. It is a story of failure by our education system to fulfil its mission to reach all learners, and it is a story of one family's triumph that came with a great sacrifice. Raja Marhaba was forced to take on the second largest school district in the country because they refused to abide by and follow our education laws. The personal accounts written by her sons, Omar and Jonathan provides a perspective rarely discussed, that of the student. You feel the pain and struggle they faced each day at school. But most importantly, this is a story of hope. Raja, Omar, and Jonathan, have taken everything they have learned to open up a nonprofit organization dedicated to helping other struggling learners. They truly are making the world a better place."

- Richard Isaacs
Special Education Attorney

"A powerful, must-read for all educators, parents and any one that must deal with the IEP process. As a family-based immigration attorney, I have learned that having an accurate IEP can make the difference

between an immigration judge or the United States Citizenship Services (USCIS) from deporting a family or granting them relief from removal. This book delivers an unapologetically realistic portrayal of the IEP process and how to avoid pitfalls with an abundance of tips and resources."

- Liza Zakour
Esq- Family-based immigration and removal defense attorney

"The love of a mother makes her jump mountains to protect them! "Unstoppable" is a very direct and well written, incisive and instructional book for parents who may face challenging issues with their young children. Easy to understand and the examples are exemplary of what to do when there is a certain case, problem or incident dealing with a child's "special need."

An amazing chronology holding a parent's hand and step by step educating them about exactly what they need to do and where they need to look to find answers. Also providing important links to organizations, government agencies, laws, procedures, programs and educational entities as well as finding resources and support. The ten pages toward the end of resources are comprehensive.

The testimonials by children and parents are a credit to Raja for the tough, hard work, experiences and invaluable information gathered over years and the assistance and help she provides.

While this may be a referral book for families that have a child with special needs, it is beautifully written from the heart and the personal aspects with compassion make it of particular interest to any reader.

A family's tribulations and courage to take on an educational system and WIN!"

- Dima Joseph-Thompson
Retired, Broadcast News Reporter/Producer NYC-CT

To book a free consult with Raja,

Email at:

Raja@unstoppableadvocacy.com

Or visit:

LinkedIn Account:
www.linkedin.com/in/raja-marhaba-5a985b14

Website:
https://unstoppableadvocacy.com/

or Scan the QR below:

UNSTOPPABLE

Testimonials

"Dear Raja,

I just wanted to say that I know when you are in the midst of building your big upcoming foundation event and have twenty million things coming at you; on top of your four-month bout with bronchitis, you can sometimes feel like you are just going through the motions to get things done. Please remember how incredibly important your work is and how many families you have affected with nurturing their children's lives and their own lives. You have done this for us and countless other families!

It is a beautiful thing, a celebration and value of our youth that is lost so much in society today. It goes way beyond the moments you leave an IEP or a meeting or a phone call. Your beautiful service continues as it creates avenues and pathways for the children and their families to journey on to brighter days. Aiding the parents to take on the responsibility of helping to create and instill new things in their children's lives, how to communicate better to teachers, the educational system, have self-efficacy and teach their children to do the same. Then as these children venture out in the world, they have tools and instruments to move forward and have successful lives and relationships. I'm trying to say, remember what you do is life-giving, everyday living in such important and influential ways that change things for the better - for the children - for the families - for the new relationships they build and continue to build.

Just remember to take a moment and enjoy and know that God, that Jesus Christ our Savior is using you and working through you. You may come under attack because you are doing such great service, but know that is because you are doing such great service!!! God has you, you will not be defeated. We are here for you! We are praying for you, as you take personal interest with each of these children and their families; you see it through and go the distance! How blessed are we to have Raja

13

Marhaba in our lives! Life is too short to forget to love and be there for the ones who you care for.

So thank you for doing both – loving and caring! Much love and gratitude."

- Debra Hopkins

"Hi Raja

Your event was really lovely and I have been meaning to send you an additional donation. I was very moved by your speaker, the family who spoke. I went up to the dad and promised him I was going to donate extra because of what he shared in his story. I hope this will help another student to get the evaluation needed. It is too bad that what works with the school districts costs so much money that low-income parents, or parents like these who got tapped out trying to help their child, are frozen out of the help they need for their child.

Bless you and what you do
Sending Love."

- Julie

"Dear Raja,

I have been watching my son struggle in school for years now. I trusted the school district and his psychiatric facility for years, following all of their suggestions and believing that they had my son's best interest at heart. Yet, year after year, I watched nothing change and things just progressively get worse. We changed many schools because nobody was willing to take the necessary steps to help him. My son is incredibly bright but he was falling way behind academically. His behavior problems ended everywhere except for at school.

The more I voiced my opinions, the more I felt I was given some generic explanation to be pacified. The closer I looked at his IEP's the more I realized they were all basically the same thing that did nothing to improve our situation. That is when I finally became aware that my son was not a priority for the school and I reached out for help.

We have been so blessed by Raja. Since the day I reached out to her she has shown great compassion and competence. Just in reviewing my sons academic records she was able to see all the things I was concerned about and MORE. The school has been so resistant to helping my son, and they have fought us every step of the way, but Raja has never relented. She continues to fight for my son even on days that I feel I cannot. She has given me so much hope, so much strength, and the ability to demand that my son receives the services he needs. I am so much more confident because I know that I am not doing this alone. When the school presents me with paperwork or documents that I cannot make sense of, denies a request, or verbally try to get me to agree to things, I know that I have Raja to turn to, who will clarify everything and give me the opportunity to fight knowingly, not blindly.

All of the fears I had in going head to head with a school district have died. I know that Raja is in my corner fighting for my son's rights right along with me. I have made more headway in the last month than I did in the entire 4 years I tried doing this alone. The fight is finally fair.

Any parent of a child with special needs knows what the struggle is like. We have all felt the pain and heartache in watching our child struggle and fall below their abilities. We have also felt the frustration and hopelessness when trying to get a school to help our children. I urge you, if you are in need of help, get in touch with Raja. Things change!! And the struggle is not as hard as it might seem when you have someone so caring, so passionate, so dedicated and educated in advocating for your child.

Thank you so much Raja. I will be forever grateful for you."

- Diane

"Dear Raja,

You have been on my mind and in my heart for some time now. Our Nathaniel has been progressing beautifully through the transition to high school, making top grades and playing on the basketball team. We are feeling so very blessed and grateful. When I look back at our journey and how far we have come, I am mindful of the people who so graciously took the time to hear our story and provide meaningful guidance and support. I remember finishing our phone conversation and feeling such confidence in knowing that I could secure the right services for my child because of you. I want you to know that I have made a "pay it forward" promise to emulate your kindness in being available to others whose children struggle like Nathaniel did. You are a blessing to the world, Raja. I am so very grateful to have crossed paths with you. I hope your journey takes you to wonderful places!"

- Deb

"I am the parent of a child with learning disabilities. Whoever is dealing with this problem understands very well the frustration and amount of work a parent has to overcome in order to provide help for the child. Since we learned the different way our son is functioning, me and my husband never stopped to try to find alternate ways to help him. The Jonathan Foundation came in to help at a time we were struggling to find the right placement in school system for our son. Things weren't going good, he was frustrated in school, wasn't progressing because he wasn't receiving the help he needed. Raja Marhaba, the wonderful and caring person behind The Jonathan Foundation advocated for my son, explained to us all the possibilities that he can take advantage of, showed us all the options for a better school placement that will match my son's needs. Raja showed us that there is lot of hope and great possibilities for children like my son to reach their full potential, to develop and flourish within an environment that completely brings out the best in them. Thank you very much for all the great help, the professionalism, the caring and devotion you have showed us."

- Mariana

"To The Wonderful Raja Marhaba:

Raja, how can we count the ways that we love and adore you Mrs. Raja Marhaba. Your heart is golden. We are recipients of such a wonderful life saving gift YOU have given us. God has blessed you with extensive knowledge in dealing with the school district and IEP process.

16

You get to the bottom line and people listen. This is a gift. I have never seen anyone do this advocacy job any better. YOU are the best at what you do. The passion you have for the children is special and something to be admired. Because of you, Justin has a chance. Because of you Justin feels so much better being Justin. Because of you Justin will be a productive citizen. Because of YOU, Justin might even go to college. Because of YOU, I can get rid of the guilt pent up all these years. Am I doing enough. I want to but don't understand the system, were the words that never left my mind before YOU. YOU are a beautiful soul! YOU are one of the classiest persons I know. YOU are someone that I want to be friends with all the days of my life. YOU are giving back to Justin as if he were your own! YOU I love!

Raja's concern for special needs children is exemplary. She is committed to my child's outcome almost as if your child were her own. And she has fought long and hard for her own two sons with tremendous success. Her strength comes from what she experienced with her own children. She gets me. She gets my son. She gets it. She is a mother like me that understands my plight with my special needs son. Through her extensive research including: studying IEP's, students records, creating graphs and charts of all the past and present history, addressing parent concerns, reviewing prior tests and arranging new assessments...she ends up having a extremely comprehensive understanding of your child's strengths and weaknesses. Raja can know your child better than you do! What I mean by that is, that the parents are not trained to know the laws and lingo. Raja finds out more about your child's disability so she can rule out things and get closer to really helping your child. She worked beautifully with our family. She has passion and compassion for my son. Raja is one of the few in the state that has received Special Education Advocate Training Certificate sponsored by COPAA and USC. Probably the only one with past experience from achieving what she did with her own boys' school districts.

She stops at nothing to do what is right for your child. I recently asked her to do a quick description of my son's disabilities even though she has only been with us less than three months. We had recently had more information about my son and his needs from the testing she recommended. I did not know how to describe the new findings. I needed to tell a new school principal an accurate description of my son, so that I

17

can place him properly. It is almost as if she knew my child better than me. The terms that she used I had just learned from her which included the new doctor assessments. Essentially, she had a more accurate description than I could have done myself. I have learned so much more about my son. She has educated me in ways that I will know how to fight for my son after we reach our goals for the present time. My son's life will be forever changed all because of a determined woman named Raja Marhaba.

"Thank you dearly Raja""

- Cathy Cimoch
Mother of Justin Cimoch

"One of the greatest gifts that a parent can give to a child is their education. As parents we naturally wanted to do everything we could to encourage, train and support our son for his future. Mark was diagnosed with learning disabilities in 2001. We followed the advice, programs and therapies recommended by the public school district. After following their program for four years we had a private institution perform academic testing. The psychologist found that our son was four years behind in many areas of his academic program. Even though we shared all the information, scores, suggested accommodations and recommended therapies with the school district they did not incorporate any of the findings into Mark's educational program.

Mark has always worked hard and long to improve and work for his future. He has never let any shadows of his disabilities hold him back. This past summer when we received grades that showed Mark with a 3.6 GPA we again had him tested privately. The results showed that Mark, a high school freshman, continued to test on the fourth grade level; this discrepancy could no longer be ignored.

From the first day we spoke Raja has been an encouraging, compassionate and determined advocate. Raja's experience fighting for her own son's education has given her the strength, abilities and experience to advocate for the educational rights of other students such as ours.

18

Raja extensively learned Mark's history, his current abilities, strengths and weaknesses. She has been at all recent IEP's with researched knowledge of our school districts recommendations, negotiating with the school team for the appropriate accommodations, modifications, services and therapies that would serve our son the best. She has foiled our districts normal policy of "If the parents don't know what to ask for, then don't tell".

Most important is the peace our son has had knowing that he has Raja on his team. We are blessed."

- Tim and Stacy

"I can't put into words how thankful I am that I met Raja, and that she has been able to help me. Raja was the one who gave me the hope of a good genuine education. The circumstances in which we met are sad, but I am so happy we did. In the beginning I trusted the school district to guide in my education. Last year I found out that all the grades I thought I was earning were just lies. I don't have trust any longer that the district has my best interests in mind. Thank you for the computer. You were the first person to understand what I'm going through. I can't put it into words how thankful that I am that I met you and that you can help me. You were the one who gave me the hope of a good education. I know the only reason the school district is doing this to me is because of money. It is truly sad the circumstances we met but I'm so happy that we did. Your son has inspired me to keep on going in spite of what has happened to me and work with what I have to build up to a higher learning. I want an education so I can go to college and a have a better future. Raja has fought hard for me; she has not given up, or given in."

- Mark

"My son was being warehoused in his former school district. Having fought this and other successful campaigns against bureaucracies let me pass along some advice I had to learn the hard way: get help from people who know the game and know the rules. This is your first time; otherwise you wouldn't be wondering whether to hire an advocate, you'd be talking to one, a good one like Raja. If you don't know the right key words in district meetings you won't do the job for your child that you'd

like to as a good parent. If you think going alone into an IEP is different than going into court without representation, you are mistaken. As a public school teacher by profession, let me save you a lot of time and trouble and needless heartache - hire Raja. You'll live longer, and that is also what your child needs. You can't "be their" for your kids if your head is in a constant chess game and your stomach in constant turmoil.

Raja is smart and passionate about what she does. Without her, I don't know what we would have done. It would have been a nightmare, and like you, I was sure we in the right, that the school district would see that, admit that, and want to do what was right, decent, fair and reasonable. Wrong, wrong, wrong, wrong. As a parent you can be all those nice things in a meeting, but either way it doesn't matter - those who don't know the laws, or don't know how to expedite them, will waste their family's time. The school district uses your tax dollars to pay for their own representation should they mess up (and they do), so what does that tell you about going it alone? There is no better feeling than having a friend in your corner - a knowledgeable, graceful, fearless friend. You've chosen to fight, which is the right choice...but there is one more...choose to win. We did. Thanks Raja."

- Rick

"When we were very worried and anxious about our daughter's special needs and we needed to maneuver through the maze of LAUSD laws and procedures our lovely friend Raja Marhaba helped us to understand our rights, coached us on how and what to say during the many IEP'S and fought for us and our daughter to get all the necessary services she needed. Raja Marhaba is very sharp. Strong advocate to have on your side and she is such a blessing and friend to us. Raja Marhaba is very hard working and dedicated to the children and families she advocates for."

- Rand

"Dear Ms. Marhaba,

On behave of my family and I, we would like to express my deepest gratitude to The Jonathan Foundation and Raja B. Marhaba for helping our family with our IEP.

We have been advocating for our child to get appropriate education for the past 13 years but two half years ago we really needed assistance. We turned to The Jonathan Foundation and Raja B Marhaba for help. Ms. Marhaba helped us find independent evaluator's, prepare for our IEP's, help us present our Child's needs not only in the IEP meeting but in letters following the meetings.

We knew that The Jonathan Foundation staff were neither attorneys nor psychologists; but had first had experience in advocating for the needs of children with Learning Disabilities and that was worth our trust.

Thank you again Jonathan Foundation and Raja B. Marhaba for everything you did for us."

- Sona

"I just wanted to say a couple of words about The Jonathan Foundation and how they helped me in trying to advocate for my daughter Jessica. Raja was a very big help to me. I called many parent advocacy organizations, and 90% of them told me to call a lawyer or referred me to another organization. The Jonathan Foundation was like the only organization that actually helped me and gave me advice on what to do for my daughter. Even though Raja was the opposite side of the country, I live in New York; Raja was there to help me. When I felt all alone and ready to give up, she was there to lift my spirits up and tell me not to give up. Raja told me to fax my daughters IEP and psychological reports to her. She got someone to look at them, and gave me advice, and recommended what test the school should give my daughter.

When the school told me that I couldn't get certain special educational services for my daughter, Raja was there to tell me what my legal rights were, and what to tell the school. When I wasn't sure about a certain legal right I had, she would fax me the law, or information on the topic. It's nice to know an organization like The Jonathan Foundation exists, and there are people out there who are sincere, that really care, to help you. I felt Raja was very informative, and she never mislead me on anything. She told me where to look for certain information that I needed and guided me every step of the way. I have a lot to thank to that organization."

- Rhonda

"Raja, I'm so glad to have met you. I can tell you help people with inspiration from your heart. I'm sure we will touch & bless many lives working together."

- Brenda
CFO of ACE

"Raja, thank you so much for helping Aaron, he just passed his exam tests. I plan on sending you more donations."

- Diana

"Raja, thanks again for giving so much of your time yesterday. It's so refreshing to hear your story and advise especially knowing that you've been down this same path. I, like you, have an unrelenting desire to help my child grow and develop so in the end he knows that he's special, his self-esteem is strong and that he was loved every step of the way. I've been in his shoes and I know how difficult it can be. I can't thank you enough!"

- John

"Dear Raja, thank you so much for coming and seeing me. You really gave me hope to keep going I just get so scared sometimes. It's people like you that keep kids like me going and to get through another day. You give me hope and the strength to believe in myself. Thank you."

- Kari

"Hi Raja, Thank you so much for all your help and great advice. We appreciate the time you spent advocating for Daniel. We would not have made as much progress if it weren't for your help. Daniel loves you and said he was proud that you were his advocate."

- Karen & Daniel

UNSTOPPABLE

Dedication

This book is dedicated to both my sons, Omar J. Marhaba and Jonathan A. Marhaba, the beats to my heart and every breath I take. They are the ones who paid the highest price possible for a Free and Appropriate Public Education.

"The Wind blows wherever it pleases.
You hear its sound,
but you cannot tell where it comes from or where it is going.
So, it is with everyone born of the Spirit." John 3:8

"But the fruit of the Spirit is love, joy, peace, patience,
kindness, goodness, faithfulness." Galatians 5:22

UNSTOPPABLE

Acknowledgements

Jonathan A. Marhaba, Raja's son
Omar J. Marhaba, Raja's son
Gerad Hopkins, Student
Mark Nelson, Student
Lois Lee, Founder Children of The Night
Cynthia, Parent
Nadine Hamoui, Parent
Dave Potochan, Parent
Sylvia Farbstein, Parent
Joy Montgomery, Developmental Editor
Hannah J. Shelby, Concept Design, Book Cover
Alessia Matera, Artist & Illustrator, Book Cover

UNSTOPPABLE

Contents

Introduction

I was ill-equipped to be a champion for anyone but God decided otherwise. Ours is a story of hope, faith, determination, and a passion to live up to one's unexpected purpose in spite of the improbable chance of success.

I was born in Amman, Jordan, the only daughter of a Palestinian Christian family. As in most Middle Eastern families, men ruled. Women and children obeyed; they did not question or challenge.

We immigrated to New York in 1969 for these reasons:
- Escape from war.
- Find opportunity for a better life.
- Receive better medical treatments for my mother's cancer.

Despite all of the medical treatment she was afforded, none of it could save my mother from the cancer that took her away from me when I was ten years old. I was introverted, shy, and had challenges socializing with people. I did not dress, walk or talk like the cool girls. I didn't fit in. School was a painful experience. I struggled with reading and writing, but never understood why. I thought I was not smart enough.

I graduated from junior college with an Associate Degree in Business Administration and Word Processing. I was lucky to be scouted by General Electric during my last year in college and was offered a full-time job in their Finance Department, working under the supervision of Mr. Jack Welch. I had no idea that Mr. Jack Welch would become the man he is today.

When I was about 20 years old, my dad tried to match me with Palestinian men for marriage. I agreed to give it a try to appease my dad.

With a chaperone, I met with five or six men and quickly realized it was not what I wanted. I decided to fly to California and stay with our family friends, the Marhabas, for a couple of weeks. The Marhabas had two sons, Omar and Moni.

Life has many surprises, and we do not know why people come into our paths as they do, but for sure, there is always going to be a lesson to learn. Omar Marhaba and I married, a Muslim man and a Christian woman. We had two boys, Omar, Jr. and Jonathan.

Omar, Jr. and Jonathan were born to face life with Attention Deficit Disorder (ADD), a condition neither Omar nor I were aware of at the time.

Like many families with special needs children, our marriage did not survive the challenges. According to the documentary film, "Autism Every Day", divorce rates for families with children with autism are as high as eighty percent (80%) and for families of children with all disabilities that number has been touted as high as eighty-five to eighty-seven percent (85-87%). Among our challenges, the battle and expense of advocating for our sons broke us. We are very close today and have great respect for each other.

I will tell you my personal experience with special education. This is a vivid insight into what my family endured financially and emotionally. It may sound all too familiar to you.

Nobody knows your children better than you do, and you will be your children's best advocate. If you feel you need help, I'm dedicating my life to helping others with this battle. My webinars are free. You can find them on YouTube. https://www.youtube.com/channel/UCxoO-ms_guLgRJPHiWfvf9g

My hope is that our battles and the lessons learned can help others who face a broken special education school system that is intended to help children with special needs but fails in many cases. We won't solve the problems in the length of a TV show but we can ease the path.

Chapter 1 - The Clues

We are never promised a rose garden, filled with every fantasy imaginable. The family shows I grew up with included problems but they could always be solved in the length of a program. I was thrown a curve ball. It started with Jonathan at 5 years old and later, with Omar Jr. at 7 years old. They were always disrupting class, had difficulty listening, respecting their teachers, learning, behavioral concerns, and challenges getting along with their peers.

In 1996, Jonathan was placed in a private school for kindergarten. During the first semester, his kindergarten teacher noticed that Jonathan had difficulty adjusting to the class and learning the alphabet. He would cry his heart out outside the classroom and refuse to go inside. His teacher suggested that I take him and enroll him in the public-school system, stating, "They have skilled teachers and programs necessary to help a child like Jonathan." She wrote me a referral letter and I took her advice. I pulled Jonathan out of private school and transitioned him to the public-school system.

Before Jonathan left the private school, his teacher gave me these sound words of advice: "When you enter into the public-school system, remember that you must be your child's best advocate. Nobody knows your child better than you." At the time, I had no idea how true or ominous her words were. I had no way to understand how impactful those words would be for the next years of both my sons' lives.

What Should You Be Watching For?

It is imperative that you pay attention to your child's growth in comparison to his/her peers. Pediatricians will let you know how your child is growing by length, weight, the size of the head, speech, alertness, social skills, noise tolerance, eye contact, motor and fine motor skills, sensory, hyper more than usual, awareness and/or signs of developmental delay. When you see your child playing or interacting with peers ask yourself if your child can do what the peer is doing. Sometimes your child may be very advanced, and everything seems to be up to par. Other times you may see a peer do something your child should be able to do but cannot. Do not brush it off. Monitor the task and see if it improves or not. It may improve and everything will be fine, but if it does not improve bring the attention to the pediatrician for further evaluation.

Early intervention is extremely important because the first five years of a child are when the brain is developing. Some of the clues to watch for are:

- Not meeting expected behaviors in the first year
- Speaking later than most children
- Impulsiveness
- Inability to connect actions to consequences
- Trouble understanding what you say
- "Acting out"
- School performance problems
- Trouble with rhyming words
- Reversing syllables
- Being easily distracted
- Forgetting important things
- Fidgeting
- Not seeming to listen
- Does not understand multi-task instruction
- Inappropriate activity in class
- Talking when it's time to listen
- Interrupting
- Repetitive, irrelevant activity
- Trouble expressing thoughts
- Leaving words out of sentences
- Trouble paying attention
- Reluctance to take on complex tasks
- Consistently losing things
- Stress with changes

- Poor coordination
- Trouble learning the letters and numbers
- Slow vocabulary growth

This is not an exhaustive list. Each child has their own issues. Any of them may not be conclusive. If you've ever attended a "T-Ball" game, you've seen the outfielder on the ground, playing with a bug or throwing their hat in the air and catching it while the ball flies past them. Curiosity is a good quality.

Bilingual children may display some of the issues on the list but that is to be expected as they transition to a new language and culture.

For more information, check out this link.
https://www.nichd.nih.gov/health/topics/learning/conditioninfo/signs

Please do not be overwhelmed with all the information provided above. Take it one step at a time. Once you realize something is not right about your child or if a pediatrician or a teacher gives a referral to a professional, accept it graciously. Remember your child is God's greatest gift to you, and your children were made wonderfully and beautifully. Sometimes, it becomes a lonely world for a parent who realizes their child is different. In my situation, my husband was not always on board in the beginning. Both sides of the family thought I was making my sons ill because I was taking them to so many doctors, therapists, assessments, and other professionals. They didn't understand that I was trying to figure out what was going on. It was several years later that the families came to terms with everything. It is a very sensitive situation that is emotional and may be expensive. Love, unity, and structure within the family is what is needed to weather the storms, not divide.

It's Not a Perfect System

Sometimes it is easy to see that a child has special needs. Sometimes it can be very difficult. I refer to this as being the "invisible disability". It takes a professional to tell if a child has special needs. This is not an "orphan drug" type of problem where the number of cases is so small that the systems administrators we trust to provide solutions are not motivated to provide them. An estimated one out of nine children under the age of 18 in the United States today receive special education services. If the systems administrators need motivation, we, as parents, need to do that motivating. That is a hard-learned lesson that I have taken to heart. I am ready to share what I have learned through the suffering of my sons and my family. I have a path for you. If you need a little help, send me a message at Raja@unstoppableadvocacy.com. I will give you one hour of free consultation. If the situation calls for more time, we can discuss fees.

Chapter 2 – The Assessment

The Federal government has requirements and provides guidelines. States define their programs in alignment with those requirements and guidelines. State programs can differ significantly. You will need to familiarize yourself with the program as it is defined in your state. The timeline will probably differ from state to state. Implementation will differ from School District to School District. Federal laws supersede state laws.

When a child is referred for special education, the school will provide the parent with an Assessment Plan. This plan is a document that requires the parent to give the school permission to assess their child. From the day the parent or the person who refers the child for an assessment, the school has a specified time to provide the parent with an assessment plan.

Once the parent receives the assessment plan, the parent has a specified time to review, sign, and submit it to the school. The date the parent provides the school with the signed assessment plan the school has a specified time to assess in the areas of social, emotional, behavioral, cognitive and academics.

There are multiple staffers who assess the child and work with the parent to obtain pertinent information. Usually, the school psychologist will reach out to the parent and ask questions. The school psychologist will administer social, emotional, behavioral, and cognitive tests. The school psychologist may administer additional tests to the child depending on various findings during the assessment and the data provided by the parent. Academic testing may be done by the school psychologist or the special education resource teacher. The assessments are comprised of both standardized and informal testing.

Standardized testing is a formal type of testing that provides a standard measure of achievement on test in a specific area. For example, an Intelligence Quotient (IQ) test is a standardized test.

An informal test would be where the child is observed by the assessor in various areas. The assessor may visit the classroom and observe how the child is interacting with his/her peers and behaving. That data would be incorporated into the assessor's report.

The assessors will compile information from the teachers, parents, school observation of the child and the data obtained from the tests administered to write a report. The report is referred to as a psychoeducational assessment report, which will include a summary of what the "purpose" of the assessment was. This is very important because the "purpose" of the assessment is what triggers the reason for the assessment. The child should be assessed and in all the areas required as per the data collection.

The report will include all the test data, summary of each test and the area the test measures. The assessor will provide his/her professional opinion based on the results. The psychologist may include the criteria for various eligibilities for special education such as Other Health Impaired (OHI), Specific Learning Disabilities (SLD), Autism (AUT), Emotionally Disturbed (ED), etc. School districts are not allowed to provide a diagnosis. They may say the child is exhibiting "autistic-like characteristics", but they cannot say the child is diagnosed with autism.

The assessor may suggest in the report that the child may meet the eligibility criteria for SLD but will refer to the Individual Education Plan (IEP) team to make a final decision. The school will then hold an IEP meeting within the required timeline to review all the assessment reports and determine whether the child should be made eligible for an IEP.

Be warned – Things do not always go as planned and you will need to record every action and decision along the way. You will receive an Individual Education Plan meeting invite. Before signing it, write on that plan invite that you intend to record the IEP meeting. Get a tool such as rev.com to convert the recordings to text.

Before Your IEP Meeting

Teachers try very hard to do the right thing, but they are not the main decision makers. If possible, ask if a Program Specialist can attend the IEP as this individual has the authority to approve services. I believe it is extremely important to do your homework before the IEP. Past documents tell a story and there is a history of the child that may come up during the team discussion. Here is a checklist to help you start getting organized

✓	TASK
	Assemble your child's private and public assessments for the past three years.
	Review any state standardized test results for the past three years and look for progress or regress on the data. Be very familiar with them as you will be referring to them during the IEP.
	Compare current district psychoeducational assessments to previous reports.
	Compare the previous three IEPs to current one to see if the goals and objectives are identical from year to year or they have been updated. It is my personal experience that some school districts copy goals and objects forward to future IEPs, an injustice for the child. Every child is different, and many things take place throughout the years. The goals and objectives should be changing.
	Review your child's report cards for the past three years. Pay attention to teacher comments. They may be important for the IEP team to hear. Sometimes a teacher comment may say "defiant", "social butterfly", "doesn't pay attention", etc. The teacher's comments may be impactful during the IEP meeting, depending on the situation.
	Review some of your child's writing samples. Look at penmanship, grammar, spelling, etc. For example, if your child is a fifth grader can they write a five-paragraph essay with introduction, three body paragraphs and a conclusion? If not, then you will need to ask why. By the fifth grade, the child should be able to write a five-paragraph essay.
	Understand your state laws and school policies – the IDEA ACT https://www.cde.ca.gov/sp/se/lr/ideareathztn.asp.

	Review https://www.yellowpagesforkids.com/
	Review https://www.wrightslaw.com/

Be Organized

Create a three-ring binder with dividers for the different types of records. Your binder should have pockets inside the covers and separate sections for at least these record types:

- The previous three IEPs
- Your child's report cards for the past three years
- Your child's writing samples for the past three years
- Private and public assessments for the past three years
- State standardized test results for the past three years
- Psychoeducational assessments
- Teacher's comments for the past three years
- IEP Team Input for any constraining documents you have to request during the IEP.

Insert all of your evidence (yes "evidence") in the binder behind the appropriate tabs. This will help you refer to documents as the IEP is being held. Study the documents and understand what they mean. This binder will be a great help for you if you have to work with a special education attorney and/or an advocate. If you have questions that are not complicated in nature, email me well before your IEP so I have an opportunity to respond in time. I will do my best to respond within a few days. Raja@unstoppableadvocacy.com. I am offering a free consultation for the first hour. Should the consultation go beyond an hour, we can discuss fees.

In the IEP Meeting

This checklist will help you to have "all your ducks in a row" when things get rough. If you can bring a laptop, you can enter the information right in this file. The text will wrap as you type.

If the IEP team states something they are referring to is school policy, ask them for a copy of the school policy before proceeding. Do

not believe what they are saying. You need copies of any documents they refer to so that you are better educated to advocate for your child. Immediately place the new documents in your binder.

✓	**INDIVIDUAL EDUCATION PLAN (IEP) ACTION/DECISION SUMMARY**
	Request Assessment Plan.
	Write on the Assessment Plan that you want copies of all assessment reports at least four days prior to the IEP meeting.
	Write on that IEP Invite, prior to signing and submitting to the school, that you intend to record the IEP meeting and this will serve as your 24-hour written notice.
	Bring a copy of the Individual Education Plan meeting invite with you.
	Bring your binder!
	If you have a reading or math program in mind that you want your child to have access to research and bring the information and data on that program to the IEP meeting to share with the IEP team.
	During the IEP there will be a note taker. Make sure you ask the note taker to include your concerns in the body of the IEP.
	Review the notes prior to signing the IEP and ensure that the notes reflect what was discussed and your concerns. Do not be pressured by the IEP team to sign the IEP document immediately after the meeting concludes.
	Sometimes the IEP document does not provide sufficient room for parents to write their IEP parent concerns in the IEP document itself. If that happens write on the IEP document by the parent signature "please see parent concerns on the separate document, dated (month, day, year)."
	School Nurse's Decision:
	School Psychologist's Decision:
	General Education Teacher's Decision:
	Special Education Resource Teacher's Decision:
	Administrator's Decision:

After the IEP

Review all additional documents and decisions from the IEP meeting.

Write a letter to the Principal and Special Education Coordinator with all your concerns even if they were added during the meeting. If your concerns were not added to the IEP document during your meeting, ask them to incorporate your concerns into the IEP document. Make sure your parent concern document is dated and refers to the IEP that took place by date.

If, at any time, you feel you need guidance, you can find help at Raja@unstoppableadvocacy.com.

Chapter 3 - The Diagnosis

At my Jonathan's new school, I requested an Individual Education Plan (IEP). Although the administration staff had given me the paperwork to complete and return, I did not know what an IEP was. Unfamiliar terms and acronyms will fly at you fast and furious. I've included definitions at the end of the book. Feel free to make people wait while you look up the terms and acronyms that they're flinging at you. You will spare yourself many painful hours later. Do not sign anything until you have had a chance to take it home and review it. If you can, have it reviewed by a Special Education Attorney or an advocate. There are low-cost legal services that you can subscribe to.

I did as I was asked, believing that the educators were the experts, that they knew exactly how to help Jonathan. Who was I, but his mother? I was not an educator; I was not an expert on the matter. I did not know what was going on with Jonathan. We were at the mercy of the school system. Everything I was told, I believed. Everything I was told to do, I did. It was the way I was brought up.

The school district did all sorts of testing on Jonathan and requested a meeting with me to discuss the results of these tests. I was told the meeting would be held in a conference room. When I arrived, there were six individuals who I did not know. I cannot begin to express the sense of fear and intimidation I felt at that moment. I found out that these people were the school nurse, the general education teacher, the special education teacher, the school psychologist, an administrator to take notes, and the principal.

Everyone went around the room, introducing themselves and their profession, explaining why they were attending this meeting.

The school nurse talked about my son's health history and any medical problems he may have had at the time.

The general education teacher commented on any academic, behavioral, or emotional challenges that she had observed in her classroom with Jonathan.

The special education teacher commented on specific academic tests she had administered to Jonathan.

The school psychologist reported any specific social, emotional, behavioral, and cognitive tests she had administered on Jonathan, as well as interpreting the results of his psychoeducational assessments.

The administrator was there to oversee the meeting and act as moderator.

The principal was there to ensure that everyone remained in compliance with Special Education policies and procedures. The principal was not always present during these meetings.

Achieving success in obtaining services and placement for a special need's child depends on how well-versed the parent is with the special education process and the IDEA 2004 Law. In addition to the law, the parent should have a good understanding of the types of tests that are administered to their child prior to the IEP.

All these people, their profession and what they said about my Jonathan truly intimidated me and all I could do was listen and agree with everything they suggested. They started reading the results of the assessments and calling out terms, like "Standard Scores," "Percentile," "Grade Levels," and "Age Equivalent." All of these terms were foreign to me. They spoke in acronyms, not complete sentences, like SLD (Specific Learning Disability), NPA (Non-Public Agency), IEP (Individualized Education Placement), FAPE (Free and Appropriate Public Education), and much more. I had no idea what they were talking about. I only knew that it did not sound good and that Jonathan needed help. It sounded like he was going to get it.

The IEP team consisted of all school-funded personnel and me, the parent. When a decision was made, it was made as a team. You do the math: six public school-funded personnel and me. What team decisions were we really talking about? Was there really a team that collaborated and made decisions about a child, taking the parent's concerns into consideration, with a six to one ratio?

You should know that when the IEP team says they will take the parent's concerns into consideration, they mean exactly that. The IEP team listened to me, but there wasn't much action that suggested that they intended to implement anything to address my concerns.

However, this IEP team did agree that Jonathan required Special Education Services and made him eligible under SLD. The results of the psycho-educational evaluation qualified Jonathan for an IEP. In addition to the results, Jonathan also had difficulty learning the alphabet and was two years behind grade level. The IEP team structured goals and objectives that needed to be met by the end of the year. As a novice, I agreed to all of their recommendations, only wanting to obtain help for my son.

During the first grade, Jonathan was only able to learn eleven letters of the alphabet. By the end of first grade, Jonathan's teacher did not think it was in his best interest to be promoted to the second grade and recommended retention. Although, this was an extremely painful decision for my husband and I to make, we believed it was necessary if the "experts" recommended it. Jonathan was not progressing academically, and the IEP team agreed that this would be in his best interest. Who were we, but parents – not educators?

In order to make the transition easier for Jonathan, we relocated and enrolled Jonathan in a new elementary school. We thought a change of schools would alleviate some of Jonathan's frustration because he'd be remaining in the first grade. His friends would not be with him, so he wouldn't have to watch them graduate to another grade without him. Little did I know that this decision would cause Jonathan to blame me, holding a personal grudge against me for years to come. Who knew that this decision would destroy my Jonathan's self-esteem? Who knew that it would cause a snowball of problems throughout the years to come? At

Jonathan's new elementary school, it wasn't long before his teacher requested to have a meeting with me. When I met with her, she informed me that my Jonathan couldn't read.

Jonathan, at this point, had been in her class for four months. I was shocked and didn't know why it had taken her so long to figure this out. The teacher said she thought he could read because he read beautifully during Reading Time. It was not until she realized Jonathan was reading without looking at his reading book. He would look directly into her eyes as he read. When she noticed this, she asked him to look at the book and read for her. He could not!

Jonathan had been memorizing the story as his classmates read it before him, and when his turn came around, he knew the story. He had been compensating for his deficit without knowing it. He was embarrassed that he could not do what his peers could, so he discovered a way to fool the teacher. It was important for my son to hear, "Good Job, Jonathan." The need for positive reassurance is overwhelming. We should all learn from this seven-year-old boy.

At the end of first grade (the second time around), Jonathan had an annual IEP meeting to determine if he had reached the goals and objectives discussed one year ago. I was learning as things happened with Jonathan. I was so curious and desperate to help my baby.

The special education teacher at the time tried very hard to help me. She told me to go to the University of California, Los Angeles (UCLA) for private testing. She had a feeling that Jonathan had ADD/ADHD. Apparently, UCLA was conducting a genetic ADD/ADHD study and it was free. It was the first time I had heard these acronyms and did not know what they meant. I became more and more obsessed, desperate to learn about this ADD/ADHD. In order to qualify for UCLA's testing, my entire family had to participate in an evaluation. The evaluation included an IQ test with a series of academic, emotional, and behavioral assessments. What an opportunity!

My two boys, husband, and I participated and the results were amazing. We discovered that both of our boys had ADD/ADHD. Jonathan was the more complicated child because he had extreme hyperactivity.

I read many books on the subject, spoke with many parents and special education teachers, who were trying to learn more about this ADD/ADHD thing. In these early years, there was no internet, no Google to aid in the research. I had to go to the library to research or actually buy books. I consulted professionals in this industry, who provided me with resources, answered my questions, and helped mentor me. The more I read, the more I saw similarities in character and traits that my husband possessed. The pieces of the puzzle began to come together, yet I still did not have all the answers. There were so many pieces still missing. However, the more I learned about my boys, the better I understood who my husband was. My marriage had always been a challenging one, maybe a bit more challenging than the average. I never understood why my husband was always on-the-go, impulsive, impatient, and a workaholic. It was like he had a motor running, and never knew how to stop it or even slow it down … just like Jonathan.

Of course, the more I learned, the more, not only my husband, but my entire family on both sides were in denial. I was told that I was the one making the boys "sick." It was all in my head, and I needed to stop making the boys crazy. Well, I am a mom, and a mom always knows when something is not quite right with her children. Nobody knows my children better than me, and I knew there was something very wrong. Nothing added up, nothing made sense, and so many questions still needed to be answered.

UNSTOPPABLE

Chapter 4 - The Way It's Supposed to Work

You'll learn that your head will be spinning with acronyms. Don't let them confuse you. As I promised earlier, here are your basic translators for meetings. Bring them along with you and make them wait while you look up unfamiliar terms. Then, ask them to explain the relevance in the current discussion.

Disability Rights Education and Defense Fund
https://dredf.org/special-education/special-education-resources/special-education-acronyms-and-glossary/

Basic Special Education Acronyms & Glossary of Terms
https://abbreviations.yourdictionary.com/articles/acronyms-for-special-education.html

Federal and California Special Education Rights and Responsibilities (SERR) laws give eligible students with disabilities the right to a Free Appropriate Public Education (FAPE) in the Least Restrictive Environment (LRE).

The Individuals with Disabilities Education Act (IDEA) authorizes:

- Formula Grants to states
- Discretionary Grants to state educational agencies, institutions of higher education, and other nonprofit organizations

Your journey is paved with good intentions based on the idea of No Child Left Behind. The programs set in place in 2004 have this as an overview:

"The Individuals with Disabilities Education Act (IDEA) is a law ensuring services to children with disabilities throughout the nation. IDEA governs how states and public agencies provide early intervention, special education and related services to more than 6.5 million eligible infants, toddlers, children and youth with disabilities.

Infants and toddlers with disabilities (birth-2) and their families receive early intervention services under IDEA Part C.
Children and youth (ages 3-21) receive special education and related services under IDEA Part B."

It sounds like just what you need, doesn't it? Once you start trying to understand the path, there are resources, daunting as they may seem. The Federal journey starts with a couple paths:

- The Office of Special Education and Rehabilitative Services (OSERS)
- Office of Special Education Programs (OSEP)

The Office of Special Education and Rehabilitative Services (OSERS)

From their page in the website, "The Office of Special Education and Rehabilitative Services (OSERS) understands the many challenges still facing individuals with disabilities and their families. Therefore, OSERS is committed to improving results and outcomes for people with disabilities of all ages. OSERS supports programs that serve millions of children, youth and adults with disabilities."
https://www2.ed.gov/about/offices/list/osers/aboutus.html

Their part in your story (and it may be the most important part) is composed of:

- Office of the Assistant Secretary (OAS)
- Two main program components:
  - Office of Special Education Programs (OSEP)
  - Rehabilitation Services Administration (RSA)
- Additional information regarding OSERS:
  - OSERS' Mission Statement

- Founding Law and Legislation

Office of Special Education Programs (OSEP)

The OSEP Organizational Chart has sections that will sound like music to your ears as you travel the path ahead, especially the concept of Monitoring and State Improvement Planning.

- Office of the Director
- Research to Practice Division
  - Early Childhood and Parent Team
  - Elementary and Middle School Team
  - Secondary, Transition, and Post-Secondary Team
  - National Initiatives Team
- Monitoring and State Improvement Planning Division

All that teamwork looks like a dream come true. It is supposed to be just that.

Statute Chapter 33

Statute Chapter 33 has 4 Subchapters:
- General Provisions
- Assistance for Education of All Children with Disabilities
- Infants And Toddlers with Disabilities
- National Activities to Improve Education of Children with Disabilities

General Provisions

Subchapter I includes this information:
- §1400. Short title; findings; purposes
- §1401. Definitions
- §1402. Office of Special Education Programs
- §1403. Abrogation of State sovereign immunity
- §1404. Acquisition of equipment; construction or alteration of facilities
- §1405. Employment of individuals with disabilities

- §1406. Requirements for prescribing regulations
- §1407. State administration
- §1408. Paperwork reduction
- §1409. Freely associated States

Assistance for Education of All Children with Disabilities

Subchapter II includes these topics:
- §1411. Authorization; allotment; use of funds; authorization of appropriations
- §1412. State eligibility
- §1413. Local educational agency eligibility
- §1414. Evaluations, eligibility determinations, individualized education programs, and educational placements
- §1415. Procedural safeguards
- §1416. Monitoring, technical assistance, and enforcement
- §1417. Administration
- §1418. Program information
- §1419. Preschool grants
  - **Infants And Toddlers with Disabilities**
  - If you're fortunate enough to get an early diagnosis, Subchapter III offers these as your starting place:
- §1431. Findings and policy
- §1432. Definitions
- §1433. General authority
- §1434. Eligibility
- §1435. Requirements for statewide system
- §1436. Individualized family service plan
- §1437. State application and assurances
- §1438. Uses of funds
- §1439. Procedural safeguards
- §1440. Payor of last resort
- §1441. State interagency coordinating council
- §1442. Federal administration
- §1443. Allocation of funds
- §1444. Authorization of appropriations

National Activities to Improve Education of Children with Disabilities

Subchapter IV offers these additional topics:
- §1450. Findings
  - Part A. State Personnel Development Grants
  - Part B. Personnel Preparation, Technical Assistance, Model Demonstration Projects, and Dissemination of Information
  - Part C. Supports to Improve Results for Children with Disabilities
  - Part D. General Provisions

It is the Federal government. You didn't really expect it to be simple, did you? But, at least, it looks like people must have thought of everything. In your mind, at the start, it seems complicated but clearly defined. It must be like this:

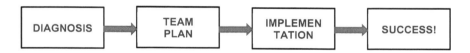

UNSTOPPABLE

Chapter 5 - The Way It Really Works

If you think you know how to navigate this broken special education system, think again! While the laws are there, interpretation is biased by budgets and, of course, bias.

Jonathan was now entering the second grade, and his learning still lacked progress. No major milestones were met. That year, I was just chugging along and taking the advice of the educators in an effort to help my son. As time went on, the special education teacher told me that Jonathan reversed letters, which made it more difficult for him to decode, spell, read with fluency, and write. She told me to read a book called, The Dyslexic Child. She thought that Jonathan had dyslexia and that was his main challenge. She tried several ways to help him. They were not intensive enough.

I purchased the book, read it, and became very intrigued with the information I was discovering. Explaining all this to my husband, however, was not simple. You see, he believed I was the one making the boys sick. Instead, I asked the school about reading programs and wanted to learn more about therapies that helped children like Jonathan.

During the third grade, the special education teacher who was helping me got married, quit her job, and moved out of state. It took the school four months before they were able to hire someone to fill her position. There was a shortage of Special Education teachers. Jonathan had substitutes who helped him during Resource Time, where they pulled him out of class for one hour a day to help him with his deficits. Unfortunately for Jonathan, these substitutes did not have the experience required to help my Jonathan and others like him in the classroom. They did not know how to reach out to him and truly understand him.

A lot of children, like my Jonathan, experience a lack of self-confidence and self-esteem. They stop believing in themselves. They are so bright and so aware of what their peers can accomplish. They cannot understand why it is a challenge for them. Age did not matter for these children. Their comprehension level was high and they knew it. They knew they had a problem, yet did not know how to express themselves, and therefore, thought they were stupid. They were having difficulty learning because they were stuck. The things their peers were able to learn without batting an eye, they could not.

Although I had a good idea of what my Jonathan was experiencing, I did not know how to help him. Since the school was not able to hire a special education teacher for four months, Jonathan's confidence level went south. It happened so fast that he stopped reading. He stopped putting forth effort and did not want to learn any more. I became very concerned, and I complained to the principal. Jonathan was suffering and it seemed like no matter what I did, or how hard I tried, I could not help him. He was too young, extremely smart, and had no desire to continue to learn. Jonathan had so much potential. He was so mature, highly intelligent, and had a mind way beyond his young years. The end of the school year was approaching, and Jonathan's annual IEP was due. Jonathan was falling behind another grade level.

I started climbing the ladder with the school district, making phone calls, pleading with people, begging for help. I finally found myself speaking to a person the District referred to as the "Program Specialist." I literally cried to her and vented all of my concerns about Jonathan. I told her that he had stopped reading and how I feared for him. By this time, an entire year had passed, and Jonathan would not pick up a book to read, or even look at.

The Program Specialist told me she would authorize Jonathan to receive one-on-one Educational Therapy via a Non-Public Agency (NPA). This therapy would be twice a week for one hour each time for an entire year.

At the IEP meeting, I let the members do their thing. They went around the room, giving their opinions on their findings and making recommendations. The principal agreed that Jonathan had been done wrong. She apologized for her inability to locate and hire a special education teacher in a timely manner. Then, she offered to give Jonathan NPA for an hour a week for the entire year. When I heard her, I almost fell off my chair. I hadn't told them about the Program Specialist's authorization, but I could not believe the principal was actually shortchanging my son. I was appalled. Only one hour?

I told her to call the Program Specialist for her district right now because Jonathan was already authorized for double the services that the principal had offered. She excused herself and made a phone call. When she returned to the IEP meeting, she apologized to me again. She approved my son's NPA services as the Program Specialist originally authorized. For the first time, it actually dawned on me that this was all about money!

As angry as I was, I graciously took the offer and left the meeting. I cannot begin to describe the pain I felt for my son as I began to understand the system. What a crash course at the expense of an innocent child! I went home and told all of this to my husband. I told him that he had to attend these IEP meetings with me, that he needed to learn about his son. He needed to experience what I was experiencing, and he needed to feel the pain. It was pain that would make his heart bleed and fill it with so much sorrow for his "misunderstood" son.

The public school district sent me correspondence the following week, giving me a choice of Non-public Agencies (NPA)to take my son to. I still had no idea what an NPA was, or exactly what I had gotten the school to agree to during the IEP meeting.

My husband and I worked very hard in our business. We budgeted our personal lifestyle and limited our expenses to necessary items. We only used credit cards to help juggle our expenses. Our saving grace was that we were self-employed, but at times, the struggle to help our boys meant that our business would suffer. In addition to office work, the business required job walks, contract reviews, and the daily challenges any business encounters.

The District would test once every three years. If I requested it, they may test more often, but I would need to justify each test. Tests would not be approved just because I requested a re-test to check progress. The problem is the results made Jonathan look very good, and that minimal progress was being made. As time went on, I started to better understand the scoring. Minimal progress is what the law states needs to be made. The law does not state that significant progress must be made, as long as "progress" was made.

Assessments are costly and Jonathan needed:
- Speech and Language - $2,500+
- Psycho-educational - $5,500+
- Central Auditory Processing Disorder - $2,500
- Neuro-psychological - $7,000+
- Assistive Technology - $2,500

These are just a few of the tests that my Jonathan needed, and some of them I would have to do on a yearly basis. You can see how easily the money starts to add up, and this does not include paying for the assessor to attend the IEP to present their report. They usually charge $200-$350 per hour. An average IEP may be two hours long. Usually not much is accomplished within this two-hour time frame and IEPs would need to be rescheduled. That means bring back the assessor to defend their report. Assessors also require that you pay for their travel time.

When the District sent me that list of Non-public Agencies for the assessments, I chose an NPA near my home. The burden fell on me, twice a week, to take my Jonathan to the NPA for therapy. It was very taxing, not only on him, his brother, who was with us, but on me too. I would take my boys to school every morning, go to work, then leave work early twice a week to pick up both boys, and take Jonathan for therapy at the NPA office. Omar Jr. would wait with me for one hour as his brother underwent intensive one-on-one educational therapy. At the NPA office, I met some very interesting people, who knew their business and truly understood these children.

I learned that a parent has the right to tape record and, at times, even videotape, the IEP meetings. The only contingency is that the parent must provide the school with a written notification 24 hours prior to the IEP meeting taking place if he or she wants to record. I hadn't seen any actual rulebook. I did not know policies, procedures, regulations, or laws of any kind at the time. All the information I obtained was through networking with many professionals and various people who were placed in my path. I believe that in life, people are placed in our paths as we move towards our destiny. These are people we can learn from, whether the knowledge or experiences are good or bad is irrelevant. Either way, there was an impact on our lives.

School personnel do not volunteer information. They do not encourage you to put anything in writing. I highly, highly recommend that any request you, as a parent, make to your child's school, you put in writing. Every action that takes place, you put it in writing.

Through my research and experience with the education system, I learned that there was such a thing as a Special Education Attorney. There was a very distinguished national attorney, Crawford Reed Martin. I paid for three hours of his time to advise me. "If it is not in writing, it did not happen," Mr. Martin told me, advice I suggest you take to heart as well. It's worth repeating.

"If it is not in writing, it did not happen."

Unfortunately, Mr. Martin passed away on September 24, 2010. He was one of the best national attorneys in the Special Education System. His death was a tremendous loss to all. I now knew that there were Special Education Attorneys who could ensure that children get access to the programs they need.

Parents beware. Special Education Attorneys aren't always a good thing. There are good ones and bad ones, just like anything else. I was a desperate mom, looking for answers, turning every stone I could find to resolve the issues with my son. I never could've imaged that we would be taken advantage of by attorneys who were advocating for children with "special needs." How is it possible that an attorney could actually capitalize on your hardship and at your child's expense?

Due to confidential reasons and the sensitivity of my story, I can't disclose the name of the attorney who I thought would be my saving grace. Let me refer to this attorney as Ann. Ann appeared to be a good person who was trying her best help me. Ann committed a greater crime than I believed the public school system did. She delayed my son's case for two years. Prior to this, she advocated for Jonathan and suggested that I pull him out of the public school system and place him in a Non-Public School (NPS).

An NPS is a private school that can be financed by a public school if a parent prevails in a due process hearing. A due process hearing is a lawsuit initiated against your child's public school district. An NPS is not cheap. The cost can range from $11,000 to $33,000 or higher, depending on the contract they have with the District. The trick here is to win! If the case is really good, meaning the child has significantly regressed, that child may be awarded an NPS without an attorney.

Ann suggested that I visit an NPS to see what our options were. These schools offer lots of programs and, usually, do not have more than eight children in their elementary grade classes. Jonathan was ADD/ADHD with extreme hyperactivity, so it made sense for him to be in a small classroom with fewer distractions. If any good came out of my introduction to Ann, it was surely Claudia, a Clinical Educational Psychologist. Claudia was an amazing individual, who truly understood children and their struggles, and knew how to help them.

I saw that Jonathan needed to be in an NPS. The challenge was to convince my husband that this particular kind of school was going to help our son, especially at $11,000 a year. It was a tough argument and a difficult presentation to make to my husband, but I needed to persuade him. He already had a problem with me hiring a Special Education Attorney. It was hard to tell him we needed to dish out more money for Jonathan's schooling and, as you can imagine, it did not go over well.

Ultimately, I was able to convince my husband to let me enroll Jonathan in an NPS. I thought we were on the right track with our son's education and that things were finally going to go well. Jonathan was going to get the help he deserved. We thought the attorney that we hired, Ann, was working for our son. We did not know the law, nor did we understand what our rights were. We hadn't yet grasped all of the new terminology that was thrown at us. So, we left it all in Ann's hands.

It soon became clear that Jonathan was not getting the help he needed. Ann explained the next step – the Due Process Hearing.

The Due Process Hearing is a process for resolving disputes between parents and school systems that are not providing required services. It is an exhausting exercise for the parents. The process is rigidly timed and quickly becomes an additional full-time job for a parent. Resorting to a Due Process Hearing should not be taken lightly.

When we pursued a Due Process Hearing, my husband and I were suing the Public School System. The due process stemmed from violations in the IEP. My husband and I were nothing compared to such a strong organization. I did not realize what it all really meant until I was knee deep in it. Extreme stress had a negative effect on our business and the harmony that had once existed in our home.

After I began taking Jonathan to Claudia for his assessments, my Omar Jr. started to have problems at school. In the fourth grade, Omar Jr.'s teacher told me she suspected he had ADD/ADHD. She recommended that he be evaluated for Special Education. By now, I had an idea of what to do, and during the UCLA genetic testing, Omar Jr. was diagnosed with ADD/ADHD. His teacher told me to request an IEP and get the process rolling. We had our IEP late in the year. It could not be implemented until the following year. In the fourth grade, Omar Jr. was ten years old and it was June 9, 1999 when he had his first IEP. The IEP team concluded that Omar Jr. did meet the eligibility as a student with a Speech and Language Impairment (SLI) and Other Health Impaired (OHI) for his Attention Deficit Hyperactivity Disorder (ADHD). Omar Jr.'s ADHD was having an adverse impact on his education.

On May 30, 2000, Omar Jr.'s progress was measured and the IEP team concluded that he no longer had a Speech and Language Impairment (SLI). As part of the negotiations, Ann waived his SLI eligibility. Waiving the SLI would turn out to cost my family extreme financial hardship for years to come. They also concluded that his ADHD was not impeding him from accessing academic curriculum. The school district only made him eligible for one year. Later on, I learned that if I hadn't signed the Exit IEP, Omar Jr. would have stayed eligible. I only had to initiate a lawsuit against the school district and prove that my son truly needed an IEP to help him get through his schooling. The due process would stem from the existing IEP that had violations in it. Since the IEP team exited Omar Jr.

out of Special Education, I requested that he be provided a 504 Plan. The 504 Plan was formulated on June 19, 2000.

A 504 Plan is a list of accommodations, not modifications, and beware of both terms. Accommodations are interventions that the teacher and the school can customize for the child in order to make the learning easier and facilitate coping with the child's challenges. It tends to alleviate the responsibility from the child and place it on the teacher. That is the way it was supposed to be, or at least how I understood it to be.

The term, "modification," actually means that the academic curriculum for the child was modified. It can prevent the child from receiving a high school diploma. Instead of receiving a high school diploma, that child may receive a "Certificate of Completion," meaning that the child only attended high school and did not qualify for a diploma because the curriculum was "modified."

On September 29, 2000, I requested that the school district reassess Omar Jr.'s eligibility for Special Education again and requested another IEP. Time is of the essence, especially with young children. It is easier to help children learn at a young age. For children who have difficulty learning, their self-esteem is easier to work with at a young age, as opposed to a child in middle or high school. We did have an IEP for Omar Jr. Once it was completed, I was told that Omar Jr. did not qualify for Special Education, but that Omar Jr. would benefit from a 504 Plan.

This 504 Plan should have been implemented in the fifth grade, but because school personnel failed to implement it in a timely manner, nothing was done until Omar Jr. was ready to graduate to middle school. I complained to the principal and requested that a 504 Plan take place immediately. I wanted Omar Jr. to be prepared before he entered 6th grade in middle school. Ann had me submit a complaint to the State of California for the delay of the implementation of the 504 Plan, so that the school could be held accountable. I did as I was told, thinking it was all in the best interest of my children. Right before Omar Jr. graduated fifth grade, we finally had a 504 Plan in place. The 504 Plan meeting was similar to the IEP meeting with most of the same roles represented.

The general education teacher came up with accommodations that would help my son. I signed the 504 Plan, agreeing to all of the team's accommodations. What the school failed to tell me was that I would have to be even more involved in my eldest son's schooling. It became my job to police him. I'm not talking about at home only, but at school as well. The teacher is supposed to implement the 504 Plan, but that was not happening. Most of his teachers did not know a 504 Plan existed. They were not trained or did not have the time to follow up with Omar Jr. every day to check on his progress. One of Omar Jr.'s accommodations in the 504 Plan was to have two sets of text books. One stayed at home and the other was kept at school so he would not forget and be unable to study. He had an assignment book that the teacher had to review daily where the homework assignments would be written for accuracy. The teacher would provide insights as to how Omar Jr. was doing. That did not happen.

I had to ensure that Omar Jr. didn't forget to study for a test and that he didn't forget his assignment book, which I had to review daily. I had to organize his backpack, taking into consideration that he is a 504-plan participant. Omar Jr. has ADD/ADHD with Executive Functioning Deficits and learning disabilities. Executive Functioning Deficits are an inability to plan, organize, strategize, remember details, and manage time. The purpose of a 504 Plan is to find ways to help him. It was key not to blame him for being "the class clown," or a "social butterfly."

Sixth grade was a nightmare for Omar Jr. Some of his teachers did not even know what a 504 Plan was. They did not know how to implement it. I ended up having to educate them for the sake of my son. He was failing miserably in school. He got in trouble a lot. His self-esteem shot down to the ground. There was only one teacher during this time who truly understood Omar Jr. and reached out to me. Her name is Aviva Ebner. She was Omar Jr's science teacher in the sixth grade. She was familiar with children like Omar Jr. and sincerely wanted to help. What a rare jewel she was, priceless to me. Not only was she an awesome teacher who helped shape Omar Jr. at that age, but she also provided a tremendous amount of support and guided me with my advocacy journey.

Unfortunately, she was the only one of Omar Jr.'s six teachers who knew anything at all about ADD/ADHD and the 504 Plan. I had to make copies of the 504 Plan on three different occasions in one year and submit it to all of his teachers. I had to stay on them, telling them what they needed to do for my son, continuously calling them to check on the status. There was a list of items on the 504 Plan that needed to be followed on a daily basis by the teachers. None of the teachers, except for Aviva, knew how or cared to implement it. Omar Jr.'s situation was a little bit different from Jonathan because he did not have dyslexia. He had reading comprehension and vocabulary deficits. This caused him a great deal of stress when it came to doing homework, writing assignments, vocabulary, reading comprehension, and studying for tests. He did not know how to study; he did not understand what he read. He would read a chapter assigned to him for, let's say, social studies, and when it came time for him to answer the questions at the back of the chapter, he would make up the answers and get them all wrong.

Omar Jr.'s teachers thought he was lazy because he'd make up the answers. I would sit with him on a daily basis to help him do his homework, which, at times, took three hours of crying and struggling with him. He would become extremely frustrated and I, again, found myself at a loss. I was forced to go to Ann and ask her advice. She told me to go have him tested, and the doctor she recommended was Dr. Don. He was a good doctor and did an extensive psycho-educational assessment on Omar Jr., including an IQ test. Meanwhile, Omar Jr.'s challenge became more evident in school. His grades got worse and he did not have the right kind of friends. He started listening to inappropriate music and his personality changed. His emotional well-being was at risk.

One of the tests Dr. Don administered was the Reynold's Adolescent Depression Scale (RADS).

This test revealed the following information about my son: "Omar worries about school, feels like hiding from people at times." The report stated he feels sad and wants to cry. It hurt to learn Omar Jr. felt that no one cares about him. He felt sick most of the time and would have the school call me to pick him up from school. His physical symptoms were directly related to school and how it made him feel. They were very real. The test revealed that he wanted to hurt himself and felt that his peers did not like him. It went on to say that, "He thought life is unfair. He was tired all the time and had trouble sleeping. He worries all the time, bored and feels like nothing he does helps him anymore."

Dr. Don summarized the above as, "Omar's Standard Score of 76 on this test, essentially falls at the cut off of 77, which is considered to be suggestive of serious depression." Imagine an 11-year-old young man struggling with "serious depression." My heart continued to break and the pain I felt for my son was immeasurable.

During this time, Omar Jr. had a computer class. The computer teacher did nothing but sit in the front of the classroom and watch the students. She would write the assignment on the board and expect the students to teach themselves. Well, those students who were smarter than the average child, without any learning disabilities would do fine. Then came along Omar Jr., and what an experience that was. He was failing her class miserably. I did not find out that he was failing until I received the progress report card. She never communicated that he was having difficulty, as the 504 Plan stipulated. I called her and questioned her. This teacher stated that, if I wanted Omar Jr. to pass her class, I needed to go to school with him, sit in his classroom and assist him in completing the assignments. She told me what he was required to do in order to pass her class, and if I chose not to do this, he would fail.

I told this computer teacher that she is out of compliance with Omar Jr's 504 Plan, and that I could hold her personally liable. She did not care and told me that she had 200 students to tend to and she cannot just give attention to one child. He needed not to be lazy and he should do the work she required.

This progress report card also stated that he had missed 14 assignments in English. I called the teacher and questioned her about not notifying me that Omar Jr. experienced difficulty in her classes. She said she did not know she had to do this. It does not take a genius to see that a student is struggling in his/her classroom and that maybe a phone call to the parent may be warranted. She said she did not believe in ADD/ADHD. In her mind, it was nothing but a myth. As far as the 504 Plan, she did not even know what that was.

During sixth grade Omar Jr. had another encounter with a Social Studies teacher who decided bullying my son would be the best way to get him to learn in his class. While class was in session the teacher would encourage the class to chant "Omar Jr. is a BUM." He was wearing a shirt with the logo BUM on it. The teacher continued, "That means he is a BUM. Repeat after me, Omar Jr. is a BUM." We did not have money in those days, and I bought most of my children's clothes at K-Mart. BUM was one of the lines they were selling. Needless to say, the class did as their teacher instructed them to do. This went on for a few days, and Omar Jr. told me, but I did not believe him. How could a teacher do that and how was I going to accuse a teacher of bullying a child?

One day Omar Jr. came home pale as a ghost. He was experiencing heart palpitations and panic attacks. I asked him what is going on and his reply was "at lunch there was this kid that was drinking out of a glass bottle and that is not allowed in school. The kid saw me looking at him and came over. He broke the glass bottle and stuck it at my chest and told me that if I told anybody he had a glass bottle he would shove it deep into my chest." Remember a sixth grader is only 11 years old, and my Omar Jr. was going through major anxiety at this time. I could not stand any more, I asked him if he had made a report at school with the teachers. He said he did because he got scared and did not want the kid to hurt him. The next day, I went to school and demanded a copy of the report I spoke with the principal and asked what they were going to do. The response was that they had reprimanded the child and spoken with the parents. They suspended both boys for a "cooling period".

Of course. this was not good enough, and now I was beginning to believe my Omar Jr.'s story about the bullying by a teacher. That same day I took Omar Jr. with me to see the teacher. I needed answers and I was very upset with this entire situation. I asked the teacher about the BUM incidents that took place in his class. He denied it. I said to him, "My son is right here." I asked Omar Jr. to confront the teacher about what happened in his class. Omar Jr. hesitated and I told him not to be afraid. The teacher looked straight into Omar Jr.'s eyes in an attempt to intimidate him, and said to him, "You know those things never happened." I told the teacher that children in his class admitted that it happened. I told him this is unprofessional and he can be held personally liable for his unethical actions and placing my son in danger with his peers. That teacher did not seem to care about my Omar Jr. or my concerns.

During the following weeks Omar Jr. started complaining about stomach pains, nausea, and body aches. The school would call me on a weekly basis telling me my son is in the nurse's office, didn't feel well and I need to pick him up. It got to the point where it was becoming ridiculous and my son's health was at risk. He would feel ill and go to the nurse's office so he can call me to pick him up. At first, I thought he was lying since he hated school so much and wanted a way out. When I took him to the doctor, his symptoms were real.

One day I came home from work and there was a message on the machine, and this is what it said, "I am Omar Jr.'s substitute teacher and your son is an animal, nothing but an animal. I am calling to make you aware of your son's actions in my class." That is all what this teacher said. The never-ending saga of Omar Jr.'s first year experience in sixth grade continued. It is disgraceful how some teachers in the public sector behave, the lack of professionalism and respect for children. Why did they become teachers if they did not care about the children? There are great teachers in this world, but unfortunately, not all are great. Students continue to be at the mercy of the school system.

At this point, I was overwhelmed with anger and hurt. My son continued to be the victim of his teachers. I tried to give teachers the benefit of the doubt, but this just went too far. I took the tape from my answering machine and marched straight to school the following morning and met with the principal. I asked the principal how teachers were supposed to communicate with parents when there are issues with the children. He said to me they are supposed to call the parents, discuss the situation and try to come up with a resolution. I told him I wanted him to listen to a message left on my answering machine by one of his teachers. I played the tape. I asked, "Is this how you train your teachers to communicate with parents?" I told him if this teacher referred to my son as an animal that means I am an animal because I am his mother. He apologized and said he would talk to the teacher and would be in touch with me. He asked me to give him the tape. I told him he cannot have the tape, and that I will be seeing him in court.

Our attorney, Ann, was now involved with Due Process cases for each boy. I had to continue documenting Jonathan's educational struggles, make necessary phone calls, and receive instructions from Ann about what information she needed to prepare for the Due Process Hearing. Ann said to take Jonathan to a psychologist named Claudia. Claudia would administer a series of psycho-educational assessments, including an IQ test, which she needed for the hearing.

I would report my findings for Jonathan and Omar, Jr. to Ann as things happened. I recorded and transcribed every IEP as evidence for the hearing. I did not have a transcription machine at the time, so I used to play the tape recording from the IEP, transcribe the tape by hand, and then type the transcription to submit to Ann for evidence. This took several hours out of my day, from my husband, my boys, my marriage, and my life.

It got so bad that I told my husband I wanted to buy a transcription machine so that I could type directly to the computer as I listened to the tapes. That is what I ended up doing for the boys' Due Process and Hearings. The IEP transcription reports would average between 50 and 70 pages. This was above my work hours for our construction company. I had no life, no marriage. I was fighting for the beats to my heart and every breath I take, my boys!

A lot of time passed. I kept asking Ann for the status with the Due Process. I got excuses for delays. One day I found out, from one of her paralegals, that Ann was overwhelmed with cases and had hired attorneys to help her out. She had two paralegals and two attorneys. Each case load was over 180 families per person in her office. Two years had passed us by and both boys were regressing in their school and home environments. I was very upset. We had a lot of problems in our marriage because I had to ask for money to pay these attorneys and my children continued to suffer. I went to Ann's office and requested all my children's files and fired her. I went home with two storage boxes full of documents for each child.

I wrote a complaint letter to American Bar Association (ABA) stating to them what Ann had done. Ann came highly recommended and for the most part really did try to help out in the beginning. As Ann became more popular and families wanted her to represent them, her "customer service" deteriorated. In the early years of my relationship with Ann, when our relationship was good, I had written her a thank you letter telling her how grateful I was for support.

The ABA responded to my complaint stating that they would investigate the matter. As all this was going on Ann wrote a letter to the ABA and submitted a copy of the letter that I wrote to her three years before thanking her for her support. Ann said to the ABA that I had just lost my father (my dad had died that year), and I was "emotionally unstable". She then sent me a letter threatening me with a defamation lawsuit. I was not talking bad about her. My children had been betrayed again - this time by their own attorney, their highly paid "advocate". A lot of other families were experiencing what I was with Ann.

Here I was with two children having significant difficulties in school. I was in the middle of Due Process for one and commencing a Due Process for the other. We were out a lot of money for legal fees. My marriage was on the verge of divorce. The business was suffering. I just lost my dad. My attorney threatened me with a defamation lawsuit. I'm not sure how much one person can endure. I prayed every day for strength, and went to church every Sunday. I prayed to God my hardest for an answer to guide me in the right direction. My pain was beyond words.

Life just does not stop because a person has trials and tribulations. We have to keep going. I have never been the type of person to sit in a corner and cry about my life. Before my dad died his last words to me were, "You are a struggler, a fighter and a survivor." Little did I know those words would be the force that would drive me to do the unimaginable; initiate eight Due Processes, four for each boy. As if one or two Due Processes were not enough. The entire eight Due Processes lasted for eight long, excruciating years.

I needed to find an attorney who would work in the best interest of my boys as time was not on our side. My boys were not getting any better. I met with several attorneys and none of them would take both boys. They only wanted Jonathan because the Due Process had not been filed. Nobody wanted Omar Jr.'s case because Omar Jr. was in the middle of a Due Process. Apparently, Ann had developed her own not so good reputation among her peers. The attorneys did not know what Ann had done, agreed or not agreed to with the opposing attorney, and they would have to deal with the aftermath of Ann.

At the time, Jonathan was seeing a psychologist for counseling. I asked the psychologist if they knew a good attorney. I was given the name of Stan. When I met with Stan, he did not want Omar Jr.'s case for the same reasons the other attorneys stated. I told him either he takes both boys or none. Stan said it would be $50,000 for both cases. I had a difficult time absorbing that number. I pleaded with him to lower his cost and told him I did not have the money. He wanted that much of a retainer because he wanted security for whatever Ann did or did not do. After much pleading, he finally agreed to $10,000 per case, and his fee above that was $350/hour. In desperation, I agreed to it and went home to break the news to my husband. Needless to say, he was very angry at the entire situation and me. He hated dishing out the money to pay the attorneys and sacrificing our home life, and our business.

Remember in the beginning of this book I made this statement "Nobody knows your children better than you do, and you will be your children's best advocate." No matter how many other people became involved in my son's cases, it became increasingly clear that I had to follow through on that.

The lesson learned here is that every attorney has an agenda and just because that attorney is a special education attorney does not ensure that they have your child's best interest at hand. Do your homework, ask for references, call the ABA and check if there are complaints against the attorney. Make sure you understand the retainer and all that is included prior to signing it.

Chapter 6 - The Difficult Birth of Advocacy

Here is where the fight truly begins. I now was forced to choose between my marriage and my boys. Of course, my boys prevailed. For the next several years I dedicated all of my time to doing everything Stan told me to do. I continued to tape record and transcribe IEPs. I began a phone log of every phone call made to the school regarding my children. I made notes every time I was called into school by teachers for various reasons. I put a binder together that was tabulated for IEPs, assessment reports for District, private assessment reports, phone logs, face to face logs, copies of school work, and homework. Every incident that took place was documented and placed in this binder. I did not know at the time that this binder would prove to be a huge part of the evidence package that Stan would use in the hearing.

From Stan, I learned that my signature is one of the most important assets I have. I had signed off on IEPs, agreements Ann told me to sign that I shouldn't have, and much more. My signature on these documents made Stan's work more challenging with the lawsuits because now he had to work with what Ann had created and strategize a way to strengthen the cases.

Omar Jr.'s case was an eligibility case going from a 504 Plan to an IEP. Jonathan's case was pretty simple as I had so much evidence on the District. In addition, it was easier to prove he needed services because he had regressed years below grade level.

Before Jonathan's complaint was filed (It takes 45 days for mediation to take place) Stan had told me to take both boys to Lindamood-Bell for assessments and therapy as they both needed intensive academic therapy. Lindamood-Bell is a reading program for individuals who are behind in grade level. I was told that Lindamood-Bell had a track record for improving grade levels in children. They could increase as much as two grade levels if implemented according to the publisher's instructions. The Lindamood-Bell Program is a systematic phonemic-based reading program that helps children, especially dyslexic children. They learn sound and symbol imagery, so that they are able to learn phonics, decoding, spelling, and eventually, reading as they move up in the program.

I did as Stan asked. I met with the people at Lindamood-Bell in Pasadena, CA. I took both boys, had them tested. We began a 20-week program for Jonathan at five days a week for four hours each day, and a 12-week program for Omar Jr. at five days a week for four hours each day.

Jonathan's intensive academic therapy cost $20,000 for 20 weeks, and Omar Jr.'s cost about $16,000 for 12 weeks. The money adds up fast. The children were somewhat on hold now because I was paying for services the District should have provided.

Jonathan needed help with decoding, sound/symbol imagery and reading comprehension. We had learned that Jonathan is severely dyslexic, the combination type. The person who really helped Jonathan the most was an Educational Therapist named Yaffa Sidikaro. Yaffa told me that Jonathan needed a boost of self-confidence and she was going to give it to him. Yaffa worked with Jonathan using the Lindamood-Bell Learning Process.

As time went on, I saw changes in Jonathan. In the beginning, he did not like the program and thought it was stupid. Yaffa worked hard with my son to make him believe in himself again. She was able to administer the therapy where it benefited him. Jonathan became more interested in reading. He wanted to learn again and he started sounding out letters. He learned his vowels, put letters together to make words, started decoding, and eventually, he learned to read. Jonathan still struggled with fluency and was significantly below grade level in reading. Still, Jonathan was reading again. That, in and of itself, was a miracle!

When the therapy was complete, to my amazement, Jonathan had gone up two grade levels, now at a 5th grade level. Jonathan continued to benefit from it. He had learned some new strategies, but his weakness was fluency. He needed to keep practicing.

Omar Jr. had a reading comprehension and vocabulary deficit. He would guess words as he read a chapter and answer the questions in the back of the chapter all wrong. He never understood what he was reading. He was frustrated within himself because he could not explain what he was feeling.

Omar Jr. was understanding vocabulary better, but he too needed to continue with this type of therapy during school. Of course, this took more than 45 days and the complaint was not filed for Jonathan yet.

We went to Jonathan's mediation toward the end of the following year. Jonathan had an IEP and I requested that Stan attend it. I had requested that Jonathan be placed in a non-public school where the class sizes are less than 15 children per class with a teacher and a credentialed aid. To our surprise, before Stan could say anything the IEP team awarded my Jonathan a program that was supposed to meet all of his unique needs. I was so excited; I could not believe it. Finally, justice for Jonathan or so I thought. All legal and out of pocket expenses were paid as well as the non-public school. I was told that Districts usually pay for the non-public school until the child graduates from high school. Rarely do Districts make parents take children out of the non-public school as the children are so far behind that it takes many years for them to make "reasonable progress".

I was so happy that Jonathan was going to get all the services he required. I still had Omar Jr.'s eligibility lawsuit pending. We were not out of the woods yet. The following school year, Jonathan started a new school. Stan recommended that Omar Jr. be placed there as well as he was strategizing and preparing for Omar Jr.'s Due Process. Omar Jr. would be financed out of our pockets since the District would not pay for him. Again, that did not go well with my husband, but he agreed to have Omar Jr. placed at the same school. Winning Jonathan's Due Process was a relief. I thought I only had one child to fight for. Jonathan was taken care of.

At least both boys were in a non-public school that was supposed to help them. The description provided to me of the non-public school seemed amazing. It stated that the school was accredited by the California Department of Education, specialized to serve students with learning disabilities and accompanying ADHD and social-emotional challenges. It had a therapeutic environment which enabled students to succeed both academically and socially. All teachers were fully credentialed by the State of California, and class sizes were kept small to ensure an optimal learning environment. Other available services included counseling, speech and language therapy, occupational therapy and physical education. All the above sounded great. Finally! Both boys were going to be ok while I continued the Due Process. At least now my boys were no longer on hold. They were actually receiving services and placed in a safe environment with very small class sizes.

What more could a mother ask for? I liked the Lindamood-Bell program and wanted to learn more about it, how it worked and how it could work so well. I asked for documentation and learned about the program. I liked the program because I could see the effect it was having on Jonathan. He was truly benefiting from it. The year was almost over, and it was time again for Jonathan's annual IEP meeting to see if his goals and objectives had been met. Although Jonathan had made some progress, he was still several years behind his grade level. Still, I thought that the more he was exposed to this program, the better off he would be.

When the next IEP meeting came around, I asked my husband to attend and he did. The IEP team had implemented a new reading program called "Open Court." They thought Jonathan would benefit greatly from it. I told them that I had never heard of it and wanted time to research this program. They agreed and gave me two weeks to review it, meet with the new Special Education teacher, and sit in a classroom to observe the program in progress

My discovery was that this Open Court Program might work for other children, but not Jonathan. First, Jonathan had severe dyslexia (the combination type), so sounding words out was difficult for him. He did not always hear the sound in the word and would say it incorrectly. Second, he spoke too fast and it was always difficult to understand him. The other thing I realized was that the program was taught as a whole. The teacher would review the letters of the alphabet and words with the entire class, then have the entire class repeat the letters and words after her. The class learned everything together. The issue was that if Jonathan was not saying or hearing the word correctly, or sounding a word out correctly, he would never know the true way to say the word. The teacher would not be able to recognize any deficits Jonathan may or may not have because she was not paying attention specifically to him. It was an entire class exercise.

Another problem with the Open Court program was that the program assumes that by the fifth grade, the child should know the sounds, how to decode, and spell words. At this point, the program would only teach the students how to read and that would be the only focus. I recalled all of my research on the Lindamood-Bell program, which had no timetable. All ages could benefit from it. Moreover, I had already personally seen the benefits that Jonathan had obtained from it.

Soon, I was in the middle of two simultaneous Due Processes (Omar Jr.'s and Jonathan's). My family was not affluent, we were a middle-class family and there was no way all of the above would be affordable for any person to sustain. Our construction business suffered a lot. We had to sell our home and take whatever little equity we had to help pay some of these bills. We moved from a very nice house in a good neighborhood to a house in a worse neighborhood. We did not have the means to support the business, our home life, and the two Due Processes we were undergoing at the same time.

The Battle for Jonathan

Before I knew it, the IEP meeting was on my heels. I had to make a presentation to the IEP team and needed to organize my thoughts. My husband, Omar Sr., suggested that I prepare a package, similar to the ones we prepared in our construction business. Before commencing any type of work, we have to submit what we call in construction a "Submittal Package." This submittal package details a description of all the material that will be utilized on the job site, divided into categories. I thought this was a great idea and I started putting it all together. I stated all of my findings in my "Reading Submittal Package." It detailed all of Jonathan's academic history and evaluated the positives and negatives of each program.

When it was time to meet with the IEP team, they were flabbergasted, to say the least, that I went to the extreme of putting a presentation together with extensive research. The school district suggested that Jonathan take second-grade reading. This was suggested because children learn to read from kindergarten to third grade. Then, children read to understand from fourth grade onward. At the time, Jonathan was in the fourth grade, so it's understandable why their offer was an insult. I told them he already had challenges with his self-esteem. He was very aware and upset when he was kept in the first grade, just so he could learn the alphabet. Now, their solution was to put him in a classroom with students younger than him, holding him back once more. I told them it was unacceptable and would only make him regress, not progress.

Well, the IEP team did not agree with my husband and I. They decided to only implement the goals and objectives that they had written into the IEP, excluding the Lindamood-Bell factor completely. I had signed the IEP because they told me to before I understood that I was actually signing a legal contract.

Jonathan was undergoing psychoeducational assessments that included; Speech and Language, Academics, IQ, Behaviors, Emotional, and Social. I needed to obtain private assessments and Claudia was administering them. She referred me to a Speech and Language professional to assess Jonathan in that area as well. Claudia provided me with a 150-page report on Jonathan. Very extensive and well written. She did so many tests on him, she scored the tests and charted everything. She called me into her office one day to explain her findings on Jonathan. She started explaining the scores in all of the different areas. She told me my Jonathan had Superior Gifted IQ and he was a very special boy. She stated his self-esteem was low, and his speech was extremely fast, making it difficult to understand him. She went on to discuss his academic scores to me. As she was telling me the scores and explaining the correlation between the IQ and the academic testing my heart was dropping to the floor. I could not believe what I was hearing. A mother's pain like no other. Unbelievable!!

I got stuck on his reading decoding and fluency score being a Standard Score of 67, and his IQ well over a Standard Score of 140. I did not understand the numbers. She then pulled out a paper with a line drawn like a mountain across the page. She called this bell curve. She said the center of the bell curve is a Standard Score of a 100, which is average.

Every 15 points above or under a 100 is considered one standard deviation, meaning a drop or an increase depending on the scoring. Well, my Jonathan's reading decoding and fluency was a Standard Score of 67, and his IQ was a Standard Score over 140. That means we have a difference of over 73 points, divided by 15 is over 4-Standard Deviation points (4.8). Every 1.5 Standard Deviation point is one grade level drop. My Jonathan was more than three grade levels behind Reading Decoding and Reading Fluency sub test. As a matter of fact, Claudia told me that his Standard Score of 67 places my Jonathan in the mentally retarded range for reading. Imagine a mother hearing those words for the first time and trying to comprehend what just happened. My son is not mentally retarded, and how do I even begin to tell these words to my husband.

I had no idea how important assessments were and even more important than that is the ability for a parent to begin to understand all the new terms, scores, and language in the reports written by these professionals. Even after Claudia had explained everything to me, I still did not fully understand it all. I took the report home and read it over and over again, trying to put things into perspective.

In business, one must know a little bit about everything in order to be able to run a company successfully so that one is not taken advantage of by others. For example, knowing a little bit about; payroll, taxes, insurance, etc. One does not need to fully understand all aspects just enough to speak intelligently with whomever one is doing business with.

I started to look at Special Education in the same way. I needed to learn more, read more, and educate myself to be able to help my children and not be taken advantage of by those in the industry. It turned out Jonathan needed a lot of services. As time went on, he needed more testing, updated testing and more support. This was a very costly process. The attorneys needed data for the Due Process.

We met IEP after IEP with the District and obtained very limited services. No progress for Jonathan and it was like pulling teeth to obtain any type of service. Listening to teachers during IEPs talk about how their children made Harvard, UCLA, USC, etc. and here I am thinking how is my Jonathan going to even graduate High School. As he went up in the grades, the curriculum became more difficult; and he was no longer able to compensate for his deficits. He became a different child. He started to have behavioral and emotional issues, social issues and his self-esteem shot down something awful.

Jonathan needed more testing as the years went on, more intensive educational systematic therapy, social skills, behavioral plan, assistive technology (AT), Audiology testing for an FM amplifier, speech and language therapy, counseling, and smaller class size. The District did the bare minimum with testing and services. I was forced to obtain private assessments yearly as the District testing proved not to be comprehensive.

The Battle for Omar Jr.

Who knew when I said those words to the principal about Omar Jr.'s 504 Plan that my lawsuit with the District would last for years and go as high as the Federal Level. Since both boys' lawsuits were simultaneous it ended up being eight years of hell between legal delays, change of attorneys and waiting for the judges to write their briefs. It was an emotional roller coaster with costly attorneys, games, financial stress, marriage conflicts, struggling children and no resolution in sight. While all this was happening, I was very busy working on Jonathan's case with the attorney and working on our construction business.

Omar Jr. came home upset one day and I failed to pay attention to him. He got into an argument with his dad and all of a sudden, I heard the door slam. Not thinking much of it at the time, I continued working. Later, I went looking for Omar Jr. and could not find him anywhere in the neighborhood. I called my mother-in-law to help me look for him. She came over and she drove me around the neighborhood. We could not find my Omar Jr. She parked the car in front of my house. I wanted to call the police for a missing child, but he was gone several hours, not 24 hours. I started to cry and felt helpless.

All of a sudden, I saw Omar Jr. walking up the street towards my car. He approached my window and asked me why I was crying. I told him because I thought I lost him, and that I loved him, that I did not want anything bad to happen to him. He looked at me and said "You mean you love me?" Oh, my God! My heart broke and I told him, "Of course I love you – more than you know."

I asked him where he had gone. He walked a good mile or so away from the house to a gas station, bought a coke, and sat at the front step of the store. An older man sat next to him and started speaking with him. He asked him what was wrong. Omar Jr. told the man he had a bad day and needed to sit and think about his life. The man listened to him and said, "I bet you your mom is worried about you – you should go home." I told Omar Jr., "That old man was your angel because he told you to come home to me. If that old man was a different man, I would have lost you forever." Lesson learned, love ALL your children as equally as you possibly can. It is one of the most difficult things to do as a parent.

I thought Omar Jr. was going to be my saving grace. I took for granted that he was doing well before learning that he too had learning disabilities. I had failed to realize that he too needed his mom's love. I swore I would never, ever make him feel unloved again. Until this day I tell him I love him as many times a day as I can. I always tell Omar Jr. I love him to infinity and beyond. I even dedicated the song "Lean on Me" by Bill Withers. Whenever the song comes on the radio, I sing these words to him. "Sometimes in our lives we all have pain, we all have sorrow, but, if we are wise, we know that there's always tomorrow. If there is a load you have to bear that you can't carry, I'm up the road I'll share your load if you just call me."

That was my promise to him from the age of 11. Omar Jr. was supposed to be the sibling without any special education needs. The years leading to fourth grade, I depended on him a lot because Jonathan took every ounce of my blood to raise.

It pains me to the depths of my soul for the agony I inadvertently inflicted on my Omar Jr. I was so busy fighting the world, the school district, struggling with the business, and trying to save my marriage that I failed to see the signs that my son was screaming for his mother to love him, that he needed my help, too.

My attorney, Ann, filed a Due Process against the District in the year 2000. We started at the District level. Ann decided to waive Omar Jr.'s rights to Speech and Language Impaired Eligibility (SLI). Omar Jr. was a 504 Student and his case was an Eligibility case claiming that Omar Jr. not only should be made eligible for SLI, but also Other Health

Impaired (OHI) student. At the time there was no case like this in the history of Special Education, transferring a student from a 504 status to an IEP. If Omar Jr. was to be made eligible via a court order by a Judge, that would open up the flood gates for other cases nationally. It would become case law and set a precedent. Please keep in mind that my son Jonathan's due process was ongoing as we commenced this journey with Omar Jr.

I did not fully understand all of the above. I was just a novice parent who wanted justice for her child. I wanted him to have services and be successful in school. Once a Due Process is filed, there has to be a mediation date set prior to hearing to provide both parties an opportunity to settle out of court. I went with Ann to mediation and heard a lot of terms I did not understand. The opposing attorney for the District requested that Ann waive SLI eligibility. I was not sure why the opposing attorney requested this, but he did and Ann waived it. I asked Ann why she did that and she said Omar Jr. has a better chance of becoming eligible for an IEP via OHI because he has ADHD. She said that the SLI eligibility was not necessary. Ann was my attorney and what was I to do but to believe she was acting in the best interest of my son.

The bottom line is that both of my sons needed help and each one had different needs and circumstances. The son that I was so sure would go to hearing was Jonathan. Never in my wildest dreams did I think Omar Jr.'s 504 Plan transitioning to IEP eligibility would be my full-blown 9th Circuit Federal Court lawsuit against the second largest school district in the nation.

Special Education is very complex because there are too many moving parts. The best advice I can give you is to be as chronologically organized as much as possible from the first day your child steps into the school environment. You may wonder why you would have to do that, that there is nothing wrong with your child. I thought that not once, but twice with both boys. It was especially true with Omar Jr. because his challenges were very different and the fact that he was introverted made it that much more difficult to figure him out. I was made aware that he may have a challenge with reading comprehension and vocabulary in the fourth grade. Many years had passed prior to me figuring that out. We, as parents, may not know, until our children are placed in the public-school environment, if there are learning, behavioral, emotional, academic or cognitive issues.

The sooner you are aware of your child's strengths and weaknesses the better for all parties concerned.

Steps for Parents

- From the birth of your child, work with your pediatrician to be aware of milestones as compared to peers.
- Get your child assessed at a Regional Center (for free) ages 1-3 (not every state has regional centers).
- There are Developmental Delay Agency websites on a national level for resources. Google Developmental Delay and your city/state.
- Pay attention to speech delay in the areas of expressive and receptive language.
- If your child has significant speech delays, rule out apraxia or any other type of speech deficit. Do not limit it to articulation.
- Pay attention to fine motor, sensory, oral and motor skills development.
- Continue monitoring milestones as compared to peers
- When it comes to your child and the public school system, get educated - learn as much as you can about IDEA ACT, your child's diagnosis, and your rights under IDEA ACT.
- If your child attends public schools and you feel something is not right, ask the school for an Assessment Plan.
- Assessment Plans trigger an Individual Education Plan meeting.
- Be aware of your child's handwriting compared to peers.
- Become familiar with your child's diagnosis and the appropriate eligibility.
- During the IEP team meeting do not be afraid to ask questions.
- If you are not in agreement on a particular test score, ask the assessor to show you the protocol for the test. Was the test in a private room or in class?
- If a Standardized Score is below 100, any score 15 points below that number is a red flag, especially if the IQ is above 100.

- If the IQ score is above 100 and the reading comprehension score is below 100, divide the difference by 15 and obtain the level below current grade.
- Review what the assessors write about your children in their report, especially when it comes to how your child feels about his/herself.
- Pay attention to teacher comments in report cards. Do the teachers say the same thing? Does your child score higher in one class than another?
- If your child continues to have difficulty in school, ask for an Assessment Plan and request an IEP meeting
- Write on the Assessment Plan that you want copies of ALL assessment reports no later than four days prior to the IEP.
- Once you receive an IEP Invite form by your signature write that you intend to record the IEP. This will serve as the schools 24-hour written notice.
- Public school Assessments are FREE to the parent. Do not be afraid to request an assessment in the area your child appears to be struggling in.
- Ensure that goals and objectives are written into the IEP for areas of deficit.
- Take the IEP home, put it away for a couple of days then go back to it and read it again. Make sure the final IEP addresses all areas of concern.
- If you are not in agreement with the IEP you do not have to sign the IEP.
- You may agree to some parts of the IEP and disagree with others.
- If you feel your child is not progressing during the school year and in accordance to his/her IEP request a 30-Day Emergency IEP meeting in writing.
- If your child does not qualify for an IEP they may qualify for a 504 Plan. Warning: Accommodations change the way a child may access material to learn in the school environment. Modifications change the curriculum and may prevent your child from getting a high school diploma.
- Remember You are your child's best advocate

Should you need assistance with your child and their IEP/504 Plan please email me at Raja@unstoppableadvocacy.com to set up an initial free appointment. I have been helping children for over 25 years. My fees will be minimal compared to the cost of mistakes.

UNSTOPPABLE

Chapter 7 - Becoming Unstoppable

We were not out of the woods yet. Jonathan started his new school. Stan recommended that Omar Jr. be placed there as well as he was strategizing and preparing for Omar Jr.'s Due Process. Omar Jr. would be financed out of our pockets instead of the District paying for him. Although that did not go well with my husband, he agreed to have Omar Jr. placed at the same school. Winning Jonathan's Due Process was a relief. I thought I only had one child to fight for as Jonathan was taken care of now. At least both boys were in a non-public school that was supposed to help them.

The description provided to me of the non-public school seemed amazing. It stated the school was accredited by the California Department of Education and was a highly specialized school, serving students with learning disabilities and accompanying ADHD and social-emotional challenges. It had a therapeutic environment which enabled students to succeed both academically and socially. All teachers were fully credentialed by the State of California, and class sizes were kept small to ensure an optimal learning environment. Other available services included counseling, speech and language therapy, occupational therapy and adaptive physical education.

All the above sounded great. Finally, both boys were going to be helped while I continued the Due Process. My boys were going to receive the services they needed in a safe environment with very small class sizes. What more could a mother ask for? There was a taxi that picked up the boys from my home, took them to school, and brought them home after school. Jonathan was fully funded, but I was paying for Omar Jr.'s schooling and transportation services. I was told that the school was specifically established for children with ADHD/ADD and Learning Disabilities. I asked about the student population and I was told it was comprised of students with Specific Learning Disability (SLD), Other

Health Impaired (OHI), and ADD/ADHD. **Unfortunately, this was not the case.** As time went on, I discovered that the student population also included students struggling with severe depression, and emotionally disturbed students. Who knew? I swear I am not making any of this up. I really want, you, my reader, to understand my pain from the system and the struggles with a failed public special education system that was broken, and still is, more than twenty-five years later.

My boys were not struggling with severe depression or presenting a danger to themselves or others. Omar Jr. dealt with serious depression but not to the degree of his peers. There is a huge difference with the diagnosis, the students and the environment they are placed in. Their peers had some serious issues, and required intensive counseling, therapies, etc. My children were exposed to students who taught my children that the way to deal with depression was cutting. Cutting their arms with a razor, scissor, pencil, etc. made them feel better. This was going on during class. This is not who my children were or are.

My God, when was all this going to end? This was a horrible situation. I asked Stan to transfer my boys to another non-public school. We tried to apply to another one, but both boys were rejected. There are not a lot of non-public schools that specialize with learning disabilities and ADD/ADHD that are appropriate for placements.

I continued applying to non-public schools for both boys but had no luck with admission. Finally, one day one of the schools I truly wanted for Jonathan called me and said they wanted to interview Jonathan. They thought that he may be a "good" fit for this school but there was a process. We went through their entire admissions process and, to my surprise and by the Grace of God, he was accepted. The total cost for this school, including transportation, tuition, speech, counseling, and educational therapy was close to $55,000 a year. No way could I have afforded this, but the severe regression that Jonathan experienced throughout the years fighting for him was so significant that the District had no choice but to finance this school.

So you have an idea of the astronomical cost associated with this situation, picture this:

- From 2nd grade through 12th grade, Jonathan had an education at the cost of an Ivy League school at the expense of the District.
- From 2nd grade to 6th grade, Jonathan's NPS schooling cost from $11,000 to $33,000/year (depending on the school).
- From 7th grade to 12th grade that cost increased to $55,000/year.

Yes, that is where your tax dollars are going. Do the math. The sad part is the District chose to fight my family, and not to provide required special education services for my sons from the start. They chose to fight us rather than to create a program and put all those dollars towards helping more than just one child.

As far as Omar Jr.'s case goes, well put your seat belts on because that took an entirely different course. I was forced to transfer Omar Jr. back to his public high school because I ran out of money to continue financing his non-public school at $55,000/year. I think we got through the first half of the school year and then I could no longer finance it. We tried to settle in mediation, but the District was non-collaborative. We were forced to go to a full hearing. It lasted ten days. The hearing can be held in an actual courtroom or in a District conference room where both sides can present. We started at the school level and went to the State level. The ten days during the State level, our attorney had my husband, son Omar Jr. and I testify in addition to the psychologist who assessed Omar Jr. and various teachers. The most powerful and impactful testimony was Omar Jr.'s by far. The lawyer looked at Omar Jr. and simply said the name of the teacher who bullied him. The minute Omar Jr. heard the name, he broke down crying. My heart fell to the floor when I saw my 17-year-old cry. He could not compose himself. It was so bad that the Judge had to stop the hearing until my son was able to calm down.

The judge gave us a 15-minute break. During that break, my attorneys left the room and my husband took my son for a short walk. I was left in the room with the District's attorney. All of a sudden, the District's attorney said to me "Mrs. Marhaba, do you know what you are? You are nothing but a capitalist. You are just trying to work the system, and there is nothing wrong with your son." Of course, I was stunned that he would dare say such words to me. In turn I responded, "If I am a capitalist as you say, then I am honored to have that title if it means getting special education services for my children. I am a mother fighting for their rights." He went on to tell me that he has a special needs brother who took a lot away from him while growing up. Apparently, he was representing school districts as a way to get back at his parents. He suddenly said, "I cannot be speaking with you while your attorney is not present" and the conversation stopped.

My attorneys returned to the room and the hearing continued, witness after witness. It was an exhausting ten days, an intense emotional roller coaster. Each side presented their case, The hearing was finally adjourned. We had to wait 45 days for the Judge to make a decision and write the brief. My attorney finally called to inform me that the decision was a fifty/fifty split between the District and us. That meant each side appealed and moved the case from the State level to the 9th Circuit Federal Court.

Remember, Omar Jr.'s case was an eligibility case to go from a 504 Plan to obtain an IEP. His 504 Plan was not working. The Federal Judge reviewed the case. My husband and attorney attended the court hearing the first day as I was unable to get away from work. I received a phone call from my husband. He informed me that the Judge called him and the attorney behind closed doors in his chambers. He informed them he was unable to move forward with the case because it was a 504 Plan. If approved, an IEP would have to be granted. That would mean my son's case would become case law and set precedents on a national level.

The Judge stated he could not rule on this case because he did not want to be known as the Judge who opened the flood gates allowing attorneys to use Omar Jr.'s "case law" in their briefs for similar cases as Omar Jr.'s in the future. My son's case would have made history and facilitated the cases for other families who were in our situation. The Judge continued to say that he was remanding the case back to the State level. He said that, since the State Judge ruled a fifty/fifty split, the State Judge had to make the final decision; sending up to the Federal level was not appropriate. This was a hit below the belt for us. My family had endured so much pain and suffering throughout this entire process. Remanding it back to the state meant my son's future would be on hold until a decision was made.

Throughout Omar Jr.'s schooling he always attended summer school and did extra work to remain on track to graduate from High School. He continued to struggle with reading and vocabulary. I worked very hard with him after school so that he could make up work and complete assignments. It almost felt as if I went back to high school.

The State Judge ruled that Omar Jr. needed to be re-assessed by a school district psychologist and a new IEP would be held. That IEP team would make the final decision. Meanwhile, Omar Jr. had already been assessed by the District and our own psychologists several times throughout the past year using different assessment tools. They administered four types of intellectual tests on Omar Jr. during the past year because the District's attorney stated that he is smart and does not need an IEP or special education services. The costs were astronomical for the assessments.

I was scared to death to have the school psychologist assess my son. By this time, I had absolutely no trust with the school or the legal system. This special education system is broken, and it takes the families of these special education children down with it! Since I was ordered by the State Judge to do this, I had no other choice. I took my son and met with the school psychologist. I was very apprehensive about disclosing information. She told me she needed the information and said she will do her best to administer the tests in a complete and comprehensive manner so that we can have a resolution. She seemed very nice, but I did not let my guard down.

Finally, the day of the IEP came. The IEP team consisted of the school psychologist, special education teacher, general education teacher, school administrator, school nurse, program specialist, my son and myself. The school psychologist began to present her report and findings. I braced myself for the worst. How would this team of six District personnel help my son? The IEP was a court order and there is a lot at stake for both the District and my family.

To my surprise, the school psychologist started to speak about Omar Jr.'s cognitive ability. It was in the superior gifted range well above 145. She continued to state that he has a phenomenal way of blocking things out of his mind as he was gifted in hyper-focusing things and people out of his mind. That was a strategy he used when she administered the digit span backwards and forwards on him. This test consists of the psychologist stating several numbers, out of order, forward and backwards on two subtests. He had to memorize these numbers and repeat them back to her in the exact order. She said he put his hands on his face and looked down as she stated the numbers. When she asked him to repeat them, she was astonished that he got every number correct both ways, forward and backwards. He scored a 100% on this test. She said it is rare for that to happen. She continued to present her report and went on to speak of his academic strengths and weaknesses. She stated that he has a vocabulary and writing deficit and suffers from a form of depression.

As she was stating all this my eyes opened wide because I knew this was great news for our case, but why would this school psychologist be on our side. It made no sense. After she completed presenting her report the IEP team went around asking should Omar Jr. be made eligible for an IEP. The school psychologist was the first person to say yes!! Imagine, she said yes and was advocating for my son against her own District. How could this be? Some of the team members did not agree at first, but then after the school psychologist stated her reasons, Omar Jr. was finally made eligible for an IEP.

After the IEP meeting was over, I turned to the school psychologist and asked her why she advocated for my son. Why did she do that? She stated "My boss called me into her office three weeks ago and gave me your son's case file. She said that this boy was done wrong since the fourth grade and to make it right." She continued to say, "My boss died a few days ago and it was my duty to grant her last wish and will." I felt goose bumps all over my body and I broke down crying, thanking her and feeling bad for her loss. All my prayers were answered, and I had nothing to do with it. What are the chances that this could happen? It was a God thing and nothing less than a God thing. We won but at what cost? It had to be my unfailing faith that got me through this and always believing, even when things did not look so well.

After I got out of the IEP, I called my attorney to tell them the good news. They were happy and told me I should become an attorney. I said, "No, I did not do anything. It was God." I would never want to be an attorney for I lived, through them, what they go through.

Below is a summary of an email thread between my attorney and I, detailing how Omar Jr.'s case was settled (I changed names for legal reasons):

--- Original Message---
From: "Raja Marhaba"
Sent: 9/25/2006 9:00AM
Subject: OMAR MARHABA - FINAL IEP SLD AND OHI BOTH CLASSIFICATIONS ON 9/22/06 IEP!!

As I told you on Friday, I was able to obtain both SLD/OHI and 504 classifications written into the IEP for Omar. I will overnight the IEP to your office today, for morning delivery. Please review it and let me know if I can sign it, so I can have them provide me with NPA associates for Omar.

I must tell you, the public school district had pre-determined NOT to make Omar eligible for SPED. When I threw all the Federal and State laws and codes in their faces about funding, they had to stop the meeting and call Downtown for permission. They were not sure what to do at that point. I believe they were surprised when I started talking about the IDEA 2004 Law, and they were unable to keep telling me there was "NO FUNDING!!"

I have all of the above on tape. I am halfway finished with the transcription of this IEP and hope to have it to you, if not by the end of this week, for sure at the beginning of next week. Something else you should note: Ms. Rich made a stink on how they needed to write into the IEP that there was a June IEP, which the parent advocate did not show up for, and the IEP was cancelled. She wrote into the IEP that had the June IEP gone forward and not been cancelled, they would have STILL found Omar eligible for SPED. I think this is a District Attorney deal. You and I both know that would not be the case.

The September 22nd IEP was PRE-DETERMINED and the committee had no intention of doing such a thing. They even stated that NPA service had begun at the end of June 2006 and would continue to June 2007. I thought this was interesting. It had to be a strategy on District Attorney part to attempt to make the public school district look better since they had so much egg on their faces.

The public-school district's head of psychology Ellen, reviewed our case and gave it to the school psychologist. "The kid was done wrong," she told Jean. "Do all you can to make it right."

It was Jean who helped me out each time the IEP team told me that 504 was fine for my son. She would tell them, "I know you are going to hate me but…"

When the IEP meeting ended, we had finally obtained eligibility for Omar and were off the record. "You know, Ellen had this case," Jean said. "She was involved from the very beginning when Dina approached her. When she reviewed the case, she handpicked me because I am a neuropsychologist and asked me to see what I could come up with. Omar should have been made eligible years ago. Actually, he should have remained in SPED." She went on to tell me that the individual who is the head of psychology had been hit by a motorcycle when she was crossing the street and died. Her funeral was Thursday, and Omar's IEP was Friday. The reason Jean had fought so hard for Omar with me was because of Ellen's last words to her: "Make Omar's case right. He had been done wrong, and you have to make it right."

Although Jean recently retired from the public school district, her purpose was not only to assess Omar for them, but to fulfill Ellen's last will. I just wanted you to know some history about what was happening behind the scenes, and when I tell you, my faith is strong, this story proves it. The way Omar's case turned around is truly amazing.

Please go get them!

Thanks,
Raja

OMAR MARHABA - FINAL IEP SLD AND OHI BOTH
CLASSIFICATIONS ON 9/22/06 IEP!!

Raja:

This is an amazing and very sad story. On one level, it restores my faith that there are actually some people in the system -- even at the public school district -- who have integrity. It is very fortunate that these honest, caring women got involved in Omar's case.

Good going at the IEP! Omar is very lucky to have you on his side.

After the Storm Was Over

After about a month had gone by, I called one of the District people who had attended the State-level case. I asked if we could meet off record at a local Starbucks. This person had somehow emotionally connected with me during the state hearing. She knew what had been done was wrong but felt she could not say anything.

"Why did you take my family to the 9th Circuit Federal Court?" I asked her. "Why did you take us all the way if you knew the school system was at fault?" She couldn't answer me, so I continued. "We did not have the money to go through all that we endured. You cost my family financially and emotionally. My children and my marriage were sacrificed."

"The reason the School District did not back off is because you would not go away. It is rare to see a family go as far as yours did with their due process hearing. They get scared and drop the case, but you would not go away. You would not back down, and the harder you fought, the harder the School District had to fight back." **Oh, how great the chasm between the School Districts and the families.**

In the end, Omar Jr. received everything the attorneys fought for, including all out-of-pocket expenses and one-on-one tutoring that would help him during his college years. Unfortunately, by this time he hated school and had lost all respect for teachers. He felt he had been done wrong and had given up. From 16 years old until he turned 18, he had no incentive to do anything. We made him work for our construction company because he needed to have some sort of structure. He was not happy, but he did as my husband and I asked. Omar Jr. had gone through so much negativity while he was at school. His disregard for teachers stemmed from the bullying he had endured in 6th grade. Omar Jr. had interior struggles with his school experience and challenges at home with his father had gotten worse. By this time, the relationship between my husband and I was not doing well, and there was a lot of toxicity in our home. Omar Jr. had wanted to move out of the house since he was 16 years old. He was miserable, depressed, and wanted out. His dad was very strict with him. Actually, he was strict with both boys, and it must've been hard for them.

During this time, Omar Jr. fell into a bad depression and focused on gaming on his computer. He stopped eating, only wore black, and rarely left his room. My heart was shattered into a million pieces. I tried everything to help but nothing I did worked. One day, Omar Jr. came into my room without a t-shirt on. It was the first time I had noticed his bony structure. He looked anorexic. I was very scared for him because anorexia was a disorder that I suffered from as a teenager as well. I had horrible body images of myself and it took me an incredibly long time to learn how to deal with it. I do not think anyone ever gets over it; they just learn how to cope with it.

Honestly, my family was lucky that we owned a home and were able to get some money out of it to help with the finances. I do not know how families can get help for their children if they do not own a home or have the means to be able to fight the educational system.

No family should have to endure the suffering my family did. No child should be sacrificed because the system is so politically controlled and its budget seems to be more important than the children.

The sad part is that School Districts use our own tax dollars to get high-priced attorneys to fight us with our own money. I bet you didn't know that!

For my son, Omar Jr., I had one more idea. A friend, Thomas Leffler, who I call my little brother, owns an IT business. Thomas is what they call "a serial entrepreneur." Thomas knew the issues my boys had with their education and when I asked that he mentor Omar Jr., he agreed under one condition: that our friendship wouldn't change regardless of the outcome. You see, I have known Thomas for over 20 years. We've always respected each other and valued our friendship.

I told Thomas that Omar Jr. did not have any related employment experience. He did not have a degree in Computer Science but had a gift for technology. Thomas told me that if Omar Jr. couldn't cut the mustard, he was out. Although I told Thomas he did not have to pay Omar Jr.; I only wanted him to learn a skill, he told me he wanted to pay him. Thomas stated that he wanted the right to correct him when he was wrong, so he could learn.

Omar Jr. turned out to be a huge success. Due to his gift with technology, he was able to learn the software program that Thomas's company was developing. By shadowing Thomas, Omar Jr. learned and grew with Thomas's company. He relocated to Orange County, CA, where he got his own apartment, purchased a new car, and earned an amazing FICO score for a teenager. Omar Jr. did not pursue college, but college is not for everyone. Omar Jr. had taught me a lesson. I came from a family that promoted college. His father only completed one year of college, then became a successful contractor.

My husband and I wanted the best for our children. As parents, we need to look beyond what we feel may be the right thing for our children. Maybe the right thing is the wrong thing. It's more important that our children become successful, whether they attend college or not. They need to be happy, loved, and accepted. There are numerous of successful business people who did not attend college and have moved on with their lives as phenomenal entrepreneurs. Omar Jr. currently works for an IT company as a Chief Technical Officer. He is very happy with this company. He gets to travel all around the world representing his company and attending discussion panels on behalf of his company. He has a lot of responsibility and has grown into an incredible, successful human being.

Several years ago, I met a gentleman at a technology event. It was a coincidence for me to be there. I commenced asking him about the importance of a computer science degree. I told him my Omar Jr.'s story and asked what Omar Jr.'s future would be like without this computer science degree. The gentleman said, "To me, it is not about obtaining a degree in technology that makes an individual successful in this industry. The question to ask is does the individual have the **"gift"** to process technical data and comprehend it?" He continued to tell me he has hired highly credentialed individuals for the company he works for and although the credentials stated they were qualified for the job; they did not have the **"gift"** for technology. That made all the difference. I walked away from that man with hope for my Omar Jr. Years later what that man told me came to fruition for Omar Jr.

Omar Jr. sits on the Board of The Jonathan Foundation (paying it forward). When the deck is stacked against you and you have a passion and a love to do something extraordinary, you will find a way.

Jonathan, on the other hand, attended Moorpark College (a two-year college). The reason he decided to go to college, with severe dyslexia, was to prove to himself and all the teachers who told him he could not make it through high school, let alone go to college and graduate that he could. I was told that would never happen during Jonathan's IEP meetings. At college he maximized the Student Disability Department benefits (accommodations and support) via his final IEP from high school. He graduated with a 3.9 GPA. He had a disagreement with one of his professors in college and that professor gave him a lower grade than he deserved based on the disagreement. It wasn't based on any of his tests, quizzes, homework, or participation. It is outstanding for a severely dyslexic college student with a 5th grade reading level to graduate with a 3.9 GPA. He also sits on the Board of The Jonathan Foundation and worked as the superintendent for our construction company.

In 2021 Jonathan went to the Board of Realtors and applied for his real estate license. He used his IEP to obtain accommodations from the Board of Realtors to take his test. He was provided extended time and a reader to read the questions for him. Jonathan and I are currently partners with Marhaba Properties, Inc. **A severely dyslexic young man found a way to beat all odds.**

They say it is our trials and tribulations that lead us to our purpose. I've learned that my purpose is to stop another family from going through what my family went through. When I was extremely broken going through my struggles with the system, I had gone to church and made a pact with God, promising HIM my soul in exchange for saving my sons and getting me out of the dire situation I was in.

In 2001, I decided to create The Jonathan Foundation for Children with Learning Disabilities (TJF). God has fulfilled my prayers.

I wasn't able to advocate the way I truly wanted to until 2014 because of the toll the due process hearings for my sons took on me. Now, our foundation provides families with the support and knowledge they need to give them equal fighting power. We level the playing field for them as they attend IEPs and advocate for their children. TJF advocates for all special needs children no matter what the diagnosis or the eligibility is. We raise money for the Assessment Scholarship Program. Assessments were the one of the biggest expenses my family had to grapple with.

TJF held its first fundraiser in 2014, and over 230 guests attended, comprised of parents, children, attorneys, and assessors. I did analytics and was surprised to realize that I have personally advocated for over 200 students, pro-bono. Running a construction company and trying to grow a nonprofit organization were very difficult things to do simultaneously, but I knew my efforts were vital and badly needed. I walked the walk with this broken special education system and my job isn't done yet. Too many families are still suffering, struggling, being torn apart and left wounded, sometimes beyond repair. This is criminal. Something has to be done. I am just one person but saving one child at a time is worth the sacrifice.

UNSTOPPABLE

Chapter 8 - Jonathan's Story

"Everyone starts at the bottom, but for me, I started underground. When I emerged, a mountain that exceeded the clouds had presented itself. No matter how long I climbed, the top was never near, but if I tried to go back, there was always someone pushing me up." – Jonathan Amir Marhaba

My name is Jonathan Amir Marhaba, and this is my story.

My mother noticed that one of my eyes had veered off during my first month in this world. Our battle for success starts here.

I was born with astigmatism and a lazy eye. My learning disabilities were still hidden from plain sight, but the crazy rollercoaster of life started with a bang. At three months old, I got pneumonia and was hospitalized. I was isolated in my own room with a plastic cover over my crib and oxygen flowing through it. Afterwards, I would be a constant candidate for walking pneumonia through this journey of life. My learning disability didn't show itself until the first grade.

In first grade, the lessons were taught through repetition. Realizing this, I would stay quiet and listen to what the other students said. I would memorize the material being taught. You see, I couldn't read. Halfway into the semester, I got caught when my teacher realized I was staring into her eyes, saying every word from memory. Her eyes narrowed with a look of confusion. She pointed at the paper in front of me.

"Jonathan," she said, "Read this word." When I didn't respond, she asked, "What's this letter?" I could not answer her questions because I did not know how to read.

The teacher informed my mom that there was a possibility that I had a learning disorder. My mother's love is something that words cannot explain, and she could not help but react emotionally. Innocently, my mom listened to the teacher's recommendation, which is not always the best policy. I was held back in the first grade. This is when my childhood changed and innocence was lost.

At first, I couldn't figure out why everyone was progressing, but I wasn't. Why was I staying in the same place? This frustration was only the beginning. My interactions with teachers changed. They talked slower to me, as if I couldn't understand what was being said. Being belittled only increased my levels of frustration. I hated that people assumed I couldn't understand, especially when my comprehension was very high, and I was very capable of understanding. I felt diminished. I started to act out, hoping to be heard. Well, I was heard alright, but not in the way I wanted to be.

My mother started getting phone calls about my behavior. She was extremely concerned. Through trial and error, she learned the education system and how it worked. After being tested, I was diagnosed with severe Dyslexia, ADHD, Speech and Language Deficits, and OCD. My mom started reading everything, trying to understand my struggles and find ways to help me. There was not a stone she left unturned, but in the end, she still didn't fully understand how I was wired.

The amount of anger I built up internally by the time I was eight years old was overwhelming. My mother would fuel it with words of encouragement. She would say, "I understand," and these were trigger words for me. My mind would race. How could she understand? She was only present for a fraction of the day. She wasn't there while I was at school. She was blind to so much to what really went on. She wasn't the one in class, trying to read three-letter words like, "the," "and," "bad," "now," then get them wrong. You can feel the heat of the eyes around you in that moment. Pressure closes in and anxiety builds. Then, you just start to see the first part of the word and guess the rest because you want it to be over. My mom wasn't in a class for special needs. She never asked a teacher what "RSP" stood for, and had a teacher actually reply, "Retarded Stupid People." So, really, what did she "understand?" In my eyes, she understood that I'm dyslexic, but how was that helpful to me? I didn't even know what being dyslexic meant at the time.

Emotions need a release, and I didn't have one. Think about it as a water balloon. If you keep filling a balloon with water, and it doesn't have a release, at some point, it will get too full and pop. I popped at the age of 5 or 6 years old. I completely stopped reading.

One day, my mother knelt to my level and said, "Look at me. Why did you stop reading?"

I stared, eye-to-eye with her and replied, "I don't want to." My face was red with emotions. She pressed the question again until I gave her a real answer. "I don't want to," I said again. "I just want to be like dad!"

My mom seemed taken aback by my answer. Then, she said that my dad knew how to read. If I wanted to be like him, I needed to learn how to read too. I lost it. I broke down. She had crushed me, but this was when the real fight with the school system began.

I learned to cope ... kind of. I learned to channel my emotions to activities to release my aggression. When pushed over the edge, I would grab my bicycle and be gone. I associated emotions with weakness so, to maintain my strength, I shut down my emotions.

Imagine how you'd feel if your eight-year-old son left and you had no idea where he went. I would stay away for hours. As the sun started to set, my parents had no way of knowing if I was coming back. I was smart. I knew the back roads of my neighborhood, the alleys, the trails, and only rode in areas that cars couldn't get to. I left my mother helpless. She couldn't call the cops. Once, she did and was told, "Ma'am, unless your son is gone for 24 hours, we can't help you. After 24 hours, we can file a missing person report."

My mom was left to wonder when, or if, I was coming home. The bike was my first release. It was the beauty of peddling fast and feeling the wind in my face. There was beauty in being alone and trying to outrun my thoughts. I had to get to that place where my mind was blank.

Another escape was being with my best friend. He had a cold nose; he always gave the best kisses. He was there when I needed him and he had four legs. This was my first dog, Buddy, a beautiful German Shepard. He became the support system I needed at a young age. Buddy grew with me and, sadly, when I was around eight years old he passed. At a young age you do not know how short a dog's life really is. The loss of him really broke me. I felt like I lost my best friend.

Later, when my mother talked to a psychologist, she suggested that my mother get me another dog. That's when my mom got me another German Shepard, and I also named him Buddy. I was thankful that my mom brought Buddy #2 into my life. He always seems to know what to do. He was someone I could always talk to. One time I was in the front yard, having a really bad day. I was telling Buddy #2 about my frustration. When I finished, Buddy #2 went behind me and put his left paw on my left shoulder, his head on my right shoulder. I looked over and met his eyes. The look he gave me let me know it was going to be okay. The love I have for dogs is so strong.

I used to walk Buddy off leash and one day, during a walk, he sat down on a stranger's lawn. I looked at him and said, "Come on, Buddy, let's go." He didn't get up, and I started to worry. I sat with him for a little while, and then, he got up and we kept going home. I put him outside to get water, and when I went to check on him, he didn't get up to greet me like he usually did. I knew something was wrong. We took him to the veterinarian and found out that he had internal bleeding from a cancerous tumor. Although it was time to say goodbye, that dog had gotten me through a lot

When the fight against the school system was in full swing, I paid a high price. I started doing after-school and summer programs to increase my reading levels. My mom had to pay out-of-pocket to help me progress. After years of working toward this, it started to get better, but I was still very much behind. To fight the school, sometimes, you must work with them, and that's what we did. I was misplaced.

There was one year where my school pretty much juggled teachers for the entire the semester with a constant flow of substitute teachers. Some stayed for a couple of days; some stayed for over a month. After the public school failed me, my mom put me into a non-public school, at the recommendation of our attorney, at a cost of $11,000 per year. During this time, she would drive me to Pasadena daily for intensive reading program called Lindamood-Bell. I started making progress and went up two grade levels in reading. After I completed the program, our attorney told my mom to transfer, not only me, but my brother as well to another non-public school that was supposed to be better than the current one at a cost of $55,000 per year.

Based on the written description of what this school offered, my mom thought it would be a great school. It was everything my brother and I needed to make progress and excel. Well, this was the hope. In actuality, this school turned out to be a nightmare. This new school was a misplacement with constant substitute teachers and due to this my reading level regressed as I was not receiving appropriate services.

My mom stressed out and told the attorney she wanted us out of that school. The school she really wanted us in was Frostig School (another non-public school similar cost to the current one), but it was very difficult to get into.

My mom had applied to Frostig School for both my brother and me, but this was a process. By this time my parents could no longer afford to pay the tuition for both of us. The attorney told my mom both of us had to remain in this nightmare of a school in order to build a stronger case for each of us. My brother struggled with depression and this was not an option. As my mom commenced to transition us back to public schools, she received a letter that I was accepted into Frostig School, but no letter came for my brother.

My mom transferred my brother back to the public school and I transitioned to Frostig School. While my case came to an end, my brother's was just beginning.

The battle with the school system was coming to an end, but not without a bang. My mother had to go to the 9th Circuit Federal Court and sue the system eight times. Four times for me and four times for my brother. My brother's case is what caused the progression to the 9th Circuit Federal Court.

Winning the war was the easy part. When you take into consideration everything it takes to rebuild, there is still a long road ahead of my family. There was some good that came with such a high cost. I realized the true value of money. Growing up, nothing was ever given to me. When my grandma used to take me to the grocery store, I would play the harmonica out front to make some change. This way, I could get the toy I wanted. When I was older, I would go through alleys to find people's trash, then have a yard sale to make some money. Even though we struggled, my parents went to great lengths and made me feel like I had everything. When the school system broke us and we lost our home, I felt like I had lost everything, but losing that sense of security humbled me. I had taken for granted what was given to me, and only once it was lost, I did realize how lucky I was. I didn't have it all, by any means, but I had more than others. I realized how much of a blessing that was. There was something else I was grateful for. One of the greatest rewards for winning the war against the school system was that I was placed at a non-public school.

The downside was that my history showed me as a problem child, and the principal at my new school made it a point to sit me down on my first day. She said "Your past behavior will not be tolerated here," she said. "We're taking a chance by accepting you."

I looked her straight in the eyes and informed her, "I was raised not to start anything, but if someone else does, I'll be damn sure to finish it."

I remember the first day I took the bus home. There was a high school senior who was having a bad day. He worked out regularly, and I can confidently say he was the strongest person at the school. I was only in middle school, and he was blocking the walkway, impeding the way to my seat on the bus.

"Move your leg," I told him. After repeating myself and still not getting a reaction, I said screw it. I proceeded and stomped on his leg with all my weight to force it down. He shot up, took both hands, and pushed me back into the center console of the bus, yelling. "I asked you to move your leg," I calmly replied. Teachers rushed in to see what happened, and we both told them nothing.

That morning, my mom had said, "Don't screw this up. I have tried everything and can't get you into a school any better than this. If this school doesn't work out, I don't know what I'm going to do with you." Ironically, that senior and I became good friends over the course of the school year.

Proper placements forever changed my life. For the first time, I was around people who understood my disabilities and worked with me to help me understand them. There is great importance in learning about your disability. There was no way I'd wake up one morning, stretch, look around, and *POOF!* No longer dyslexic. Dyslexia is something that I will live with my whole life. The most important thing that came from understanding my disabilities is that I was able to start finding ways to cope with them. I quickly found out I could turn this disability into a strength. Once I developed that deeper understanding, I was able to work toward success.

Let's get something straight. I don't like the word "disability." That word has a very negative connotation. My so-called "disability" has been my greatest gift. For example, if you and I were both given something to read, you could see it once, get it, and throw it aside. I would have to look it over, hopefully, get the title, then a second time to maybe get a couple words in the first sentence, then a third time, to hopefully get a couple more sentences and work my way through it. Now, even though it took me much longer than you to review it, I have a deeper understanding of the material because of it. If you and I had to discuss the information, I would have an advantage over you, all thanks to this so-called disability, my dyslexia.

I also got back in touch with my love for acting. I had an amazing drama teacher, Christina, who wanted me in her drama class. I shied away and wanted to stay in pottery because I enjoyed throwing clay. Christina was persistent and made sure that I ended up in drama class against my will.

The first day in the elective, Christina took me aside and told me, "Jonathan, you can change electives if you really wanted to, but I really want you to be a part of the next play."

I felt safe and I decided to stay with drama. I ended up falling in love with the stage. From that day forward, I performed in every play until I graduated. A thank you doesn't do her justice for what she did for me. She helped boost my confidence and showed me how much I loved acting.

I learned mental strength in a gym at 17 years old, leg pressing 1200 lbs. One day, I was alone in the gym. I laid on the press to begin my routine. I used to rep with that weight with no problem, but that day, something was different. Towards the end of the workout, I was tired and started to doubt my ability to finish. I gave up on myself and watched as the weight slowly lowered towards me. As it drew near, something snapped inside of me. "What's wrong with you?" I asked myself. "I rep this all the time. This isn't shit... It's not even my max. LET'S GO!" Out of nowhere, I threw the weight up, as if it was nothing, and racked it. From that point on, I realized the importance of mental strength and how it can either be your greatest asset or your worst enemy.

College was a challenge, but I had accommodations, which made a world of difference. In college I went to the Disabled Student's Program Services (DSPS) so that I can implement the IEP accommodations I had in High School at the college level. This allowed me to have all my textbooks digitally and provided me with a reading software (Kurzweil) that read all literature to me. I was provided a note taker and had a private room with a computer for test taking. For some literature exams, the teacher required the essays all be handwritten. In order to accommodate this the DSPS office assigned somebody to transcribe my typed essay into a written word. Lastly, I was provided double time on test taking.

The IEP was another gift I received from my family's fight with the school system. I also learned how to self-advocate, something that only came after I learned how my disability affected me. It helped me build the self-confidence to do what I needed to do at the college level.

Because of a surgery, I missed my accounting class. Although I had notified my teacher verbally and by email prior to the surgery, I was never told about a test in that class. When I returned to class with my arm in a sling, the teacher made a comment about how I missed the test.

"Is it possible for me to take the test last?" I asked my professor.

"You read my syllabus – no exceptions. You will take a zero for it," He replied.

I tried to plead my case to him, but he shut down everything I said. In the middle of class, I stood up, grabbed my stuff, and walked out. I went straight to his dean with emailed proof to plead my case.

"He's been here for a while," the Dean said, "and no one has ever complained about him. It doesn't sound like him."

"My GPA is a 4.0," I told her. "Do you really think I would be lying? Maybe no one cared enough to come talk to you. Have you ever thought about that?" I ended up getting an extension for the test. During the test, I found a mistake the accounting teacher had made, which resulted in me scoring 110%. I finished that class with an A.

As my college career came closer to an end, I decided to take another drama class. This would change my life. My drama teacher was an amazing woman named Peggy. When she found out that I had done plays in high school, she pushed me to audition for an upcoming play. I joked about doing it but blew off the audition. The next class meeting, she asked me if I auditioned. I respectfully told here that I had missed auditions, but that wasn't going to be acceptable to her. Peggy looked at me and said, "You're going to audition for the play after class today. Do I need to personally walk you over there?"

Needless to say, I auditioned for the play after Peggy's convincing and to my surprise, I landed a role. It re-sparked the love I had for acting, brought amazing people into my life, and helped me understand why certain things happened in my life.

I had the hardest time understanding how I had so much raw talent in football, but never got to let it really shine. Three years after high school I returned to Frostig School to show support for my high school team and to just visit the kids, give back any way I could. A rival team's coach approached me at the game and asked where I was playing football in college. When I told him my career in football was over, explaining that I had permanently damaged my shoulder, I could see the sadness in his eyes. He exhaled deeply and said, "You were special."

On the same night I was set to perform in one of our last plays of the semester, there was a football game down the hill. I walked out to my car before the play started and could hear the crowd. For a moment, I sat on the curb, looking down at the field and hearing some names I knew. It hurt that I couldn't be out there. I couldn't go into battle with them. Feeling a little down, I got ready for the play.

The performance that night felt so good. I remember walking on stage and then, nothing. I was so deep in my character; the play just passed me by. I had a great performance and won a different battle. The man upstairs had an alternate path for me. Because of injuries, football wasn't part of his plan.

After graduation, I needed to do something with myself, so I did the one thing I knew. I stepped back into the world of construction. I started with doing grunt work. I wanted to start at the bottom and earn my spot.

While on a particular project, there was a superintendent who wasn't doing his duties. Naturally, I started to pick up the slack. I ended up finishing that job for him and was given an opportunity to be the superintendent on the next project. Eager to learn, I stepped into the role. Little did I know, this would be the biggest project the company had done. I had to deal with multiple trades. From that opportunity, I was sent for OSHA training and QC qualifications. I started running multiple projects, and soon, became successful in my trade. I knew that experience was a great steppingstone on the journey to success, but for me, there was something bigger.

Our trials and tribulations pushed my mother to establish a non-profit, The Jonathan Foundation for Children with Learning Disabilities. We quickly concluded that no one should have to suffer the way we had suffered to get what was supposed to be a Free and Appropriate Public Education. While we fought the education system, we had multiple organizations turn us away because we didn't fall into the criteria of the target population they helped. We wanted to cut all the red tape.

The first taste of accomplishment I felt was when a young man who was born without sweat glands came to the foundation. His parents feared for his life in the public school system. My mother researched his diagnosis and helped fight for him. She was able to get him a non-public School placement. He and I went to the same high school and I'll never forget what he told me one day when I was at the school for a visit, "Your mom is my angel. Tell her thank you."

My passion for the foundation comes from my past. I realized that there were people in my life who had changed it for the better. I know that I wouldn't be where I am today if I had not encountered those individuals. My high school teacher, Jason, is one of those people. He always helped push me and expand my vocabulary. He was able to get a dyslexic person to read books and knew how to engage me, but it goes deeper than that. My high school sent me to mediator training, and through this, I was presented with a scholarship opportunity.

It required writing a paper. The staff at my high school were all very encouraging and gave up personal time to help me edit the paper. Yes, personal time! I remember, right before the due date, I spent time after school in Jason's class. He gave up his time to review my essay because he knew writing was a weakness for me. He understood my disabilities. He gave something up to help promote my success. Once my eyes opened, I realized how many teachers really gave more than required because it came from their hearts. They recognized that there is something greater than money. I learned this first hand. To the principal and teachers at Frostig School who helped me from middle school through high school, Thank you!

I mentor children for the foundation my mom started, and my goal is to save these kids. I am a rare case and was able to experience all sides of the ball from the good, the bad, the ugly, and even as a spectator. I was able to stand back and watch parents interact with their kids. I saw the root of their frustration and watched how disconnected parents and their children truly were. My mother and I had the same disconnect for a very long time. A main part of it was the difference between telling and showing. As a parent, you naturally tell your child what to do and give direct orders. This trend builds unhealthy habits when parents try to communicate with their child. I want to show you what I mean by this.

If you recall, my trigger words are "I understand." That phrase was the root of extreme frustration for me and caused me to shut down. In my mother's eyes, the phrase was her way of giving me words of encouragement. When showing someone that you understand, there is a different approach. I realized that when I was going through an emotional rollercoaster. I would alienate myself and feel a sense of loneliness. I thought there was no one out there going through what I was going through. Everyone who tried to reach out was shut out because they assumed they knew how to get to me. In my eyes, their so-called "knowing" was only scratching the surface.

Since I know this about myself, when I talk to kids, I try to take the "showing" approach. I listen very intently, seeing where I can open up about myself, become vulnerable, and share some of my hardship with them. I explain how I felt when I was their age or going through my toughest times to see if it parallels with the child. I avoid being subjective, assuming how they feel, and instead, wait for them to volunteer that notion. When doing this, I find myself building rapport, allowing them to feel comfortable enough to open up more. By presenting my story, I find ways of building a deeper trust and letting them know that even with all the hardship, I was still able to be successful.

I had several challenges throughout my construction career because I had to earn my stripes. Being 23 to 24 years old, a lot of subcontractors had little respect for me due to my age, and what they felt was a lack of experience. I had some good subcontractors I worked with who took the time and helped me get to speed.

After all the hardships my parents endured fighting the school system and trying to keep the construction business afloat, it took a huge toll on their marriage. They separated, living in different homes yet working together in the business.

Both were going through extreme stress. My mom told me to be her eyes in the field as she ran operations in the office. My mom and dad were not as motivated as they once were about the business. Both had to protect the business from the subcontractors, employees, clients, and vendors finding out that the marriage was in trouble. They did not want the current situation to be made public, afraid that it would impact the business negatively. There was too much at risk and as much as they both were trying to do the right things, sometimes, they fell short.

My dad did the best he could in the field, but of course, both parent's emotional state of mind was not conducive. I became a full time Superintendent and had a couple of projects under my belt. There was a project where a Federal Project Manager came up to me and stated, "Get me a new Project Manager because this one is not working for me." I was my mom's eyes in the field, and the field was struggling. This forced me to become a Superintendent/Project Manager. I was able to step up in many ways to strengthen the field and complete the project successfully. I reported to my mom all I could so she can keep the company going as smooth as possible on paper, while I did my best to help in the field and support my dad.

This forced me to grow and take over more responsibilities. I had a new goal now, I needed to retire my mom from construction. She never loved construction, but circumstances beyond her control forced her into it. She gave up her corporate career to build a business with my dad for a better future. As much as she wanted out of the business she could not quit because she signed all the contracts with the government and was obligated to finish out the contract for the remaining years.

We decided that we would end construction with a bang. By this time, I was 28 years old, and running multiple multimillion-dollar projects, simultaneously. I even had other companies coming after me, saying "I know you work for your family but tell me what number to put on a check to make you come work for us." This was very humbling for me because there were not a lot of people my age that had the ability to comprehend architectural drawings, manage subcontractors and employees on various projects, work with engineers, and attend high profile meetings with clients. By the end of our journey to close the company I had realized that the experience I gained by being thrown into an ocean without a life vest and told to swim was the best thing that could have happened to me. I went through an incredible learning curve and lessons that will benefit me in my future endeavors.

The dust finally settled. We completed all of our projects and said good-bye to construction. I was really good at it but wanted something more. In 2012, I was ready to get my real-estate license, but, with my parent's challenges with the marriage and the business, I had to put my real estate career on hold. Luckily, I was still eligible to take my state exam for my license due to Covid and the Board of Realtor's extending my eligibility requirement for test taking. I got my real estate license in 2021. I commenced with residential real estate, but my true love is commercial. I figured with my extensive commercial construction experience commercial real estate would be a good fit for me. I started my own real estate company, Marhaba Properties, Inc. and donate part of my commission back to nonprofits. I feel there is a gift in giving back, and I want to show that to my clients. I want them to see firsthand the impact they made through my contribution.

Success is a goal only limited by your drive and aspirations. I became the friend people can always call on if they need anything. **There is something greater than the value of a dollar; it is the ability to change a person's life.** When a child comes back to me and says, "You've changed my life. I wouldn't be where I am today if it wasn't for you. Thank you," that's the greatest gift in this world. I have the ability to change a life. The most beautiful part about it is that the people I help might take what I give them and perpetuate that to the next person. How amazing would it be to start a domino effect of change?

Chapter 9 - Omar's Story

I don't remember much from when I was little. A majority of it I blocked out. I remember my parents were always working. I don't remember seeing my dad much, except when we did family trips. Most of my childhood memories are of my brother and I swimming at my grandparents' house. My parents had us in sports since before I can remember. We played baseball, basketball, and football. Sometimes, we would leave a football game to go to basketball practice. My poor mom did a lot for us ... she still does.

I loved sports, especially football. My childhood dream was always to be good enough to play for UCLA. Why UCLA? I have no idea. But my heart was set on playing for them. Growing up, I was always a star athlete. My little brother was always overshadowed by my capabilities. When we were younger, he struggled with a lot. I didn't understand it much then, but I have a much better understanding now and greater respect for everything he was able to achieve.

Growing up, my favorite part of school was P.E. I loved to do activities and was never really able to sit still. One day in 6th grade, school went from something tolerable to a nightmare. I was bullied by my teacher in front of my peers. Even today, the thought still angers me. During that time, I was extremely hurt and embarrassed. I could no longer even step foot in the class.

Teachers did not understand me and did not treat me with kindness. I had a computer teacher who told my mom she needed to sit in my class with me in order for me to pass her class because she did not have time for me with her 200-student caseload. There was only one teacher that truly cared about me, and her name is Aviva Ebner. She reached out to me in middle school when no other teacher cared. She showed kindness, patience, and compassion. She understood me. I am not sure if she truly knows how much she impacted me during such darkness in my life. She is, and continues to be, the only teacher that I truly love and respect.

I struggled in school. I had poor reading comprehension and vocabulary. I was always frustrated and felt like an idiot when I couldn't retain the same information from a story that most of my peers could. This affected all of my classes.

After being bullied, on top of all my other struggles, I became a broken child. My mom saw this and did everything she could to get me the help she believed was needed for me to succeed. My dad, on the other hand, didn't understand it. His views were the same as everyone else's. I was a troubled child, but the calls for help I created must've looked like the antics of a disobedient child, looking to cause mischief.

When I was in 8th grade, I completed a math assignment without showing the work. My teacher told me that even though my answer was correct, she marked it wrong because I did not show my work. It took longer to show my work, but I was able to get the right answer in my head faster, so I refused to waste time showing work. It made no sense to me at the time. My punishment was to sit in front of the principal's office for the remainder of the day and work on the assignment, showing my work. I grew extremely frustrated and shredded the hardcover math book in retaliation.

Fast forward a few years, we were moving from school to school, home to home, the one thing I lacked in life was a form of stability. Now that I'm older, it's the one thing I want out of life. I'm not there just yet, but I'm much closer than I have ever been.

Going through high school, I was finally given the help I needed to assist me with my studies. I did better in classes, however, it took away from the one thing I loved the most – playing sports, specifically football.

I always looked up to my dad. He was the person I strived to be like and my coach. When I told my dad I wanted to play football at school, he told me he didn't think I had the attitude for it. You see my dad was a huge fan of the game, competitive and very tough, not only on me, but on my brother as well. He was not a bad father as he worked extremely hard to provide for us. He was a Middle Eastern man, raised a certain way and the belief is to raise children with an iron fist. He tried to be there for the practice games, and made it a point to be there for most of the games. One year he even became a coach. My dad was my life coach and he had just told me he didn't have faith in my ability. So, instead of pursuing football, I left school and walked to the park by the house, where I played basketball until late at night.

It was my getaway from reality. I didn't have to worry about what anyone thought. I still had to do schoolwork, but I just didn't do it. I just played basketball. One day, a friend of mine introduced me to a LAN center. It's a computer café without the café. In about thirty minutes, I got addicted to *Counter-strike*. Once I went home, I asked my mom to get the game for me. She kindly did, not knowing anything about it. I hadn't used the computer my parents had gotten for me (to use for schoolwork) until now. I loved *Counter-strike.* It was competitive and I was good at it. The problem was that my computer at the time was not able to run well enough to really compete in the game.

At 14, I told my mom I wanted to build a computer. She asked me if I knew how and I told her I did. I did all the research and used her credit card to buy the parts. My dad thought I was going to need his help. He was skeptical because I was very young, and he truly did not know my gift with computers. Within a week, multiple boxes were shipped to the house. My parents weren't exactly sure if I knew what I was doing. Once I received all the parts, within a couple hours, I was playing on my new computer. It was an amazing feeling, especially since I could game without issues. My dad was impressed to say the least. He did not think I could do it, but was very proud of me in the end.

I played a lot… it was excessive. I was still able to get what I needed done for school, but gaming slowly became my place to run from the world, instead of sports. When I finished high school, my dad gave me two choices that I will never forget: 1) you go to college; or 2) you work for me. The reason he made such a statement was because I had no desire to go to college and college was very important for our family. Both parents told me without a college degree I will not be able to get a good paying job. I hated school and authority because of my horrible experience with teachers. The teacher I have the most respect for was Aviva, my science teacher. She did everything in her power to keep me on the right track.

My parents owned a construction company. Since I was done with school, I decided to become an electrician and work with my dad. I joined an apprenticeship program, which allowed me to make good money. Initially, working was great. Then it turned into hell. My dad was an incredible businessman. However, he did not know how to mentor employees and, like most entrepreneurs, letting go of work and delegating duties was difficult for him. My dad never had a mentor to show him the ropes. How could he know how to mentor others?

At 17, this was a lot of stress and pressure for me. Work never ended for me. Once I finished work and clocked out, I had to get my truck ready, then go home and talk about work with my dad. It felt like I was always working, which caused more conflict between my dad and I. This also triggered me into spending more time playing games. I couldn't hear him with my headset on.

With my mom fighting the schools to get my brother the help he needed and the growing tensions between my dad and I, our family was greatly impacted. My parents separated in 2007. It was extremely difficult and upsetting to have to do electrical work on a house that my mom was moving into. My mom was no longer home to help mediate the relationship between my dad and I, so tensions continued to grow.

One day, at work, I got injured and nearly cut off my left thumb. After that day, I decided I was never doing construction again and started looking for other work to do. Since I had stopped working completely, it caused issues at home with my dad. I was picky about finding a career. My dad didn't understand that and complained. I went on interviews for different jobs but ended up turning them all down because I wasn't interested. I was doing the footwork to show that I wasn't at home playing games all day.

This approach worked for a short time, but then, my dad told me I had to do something with my life. Looking back, from his perspective, he wasn't wrong. His approach was the problem, but it did look like all I wanted to do was sit at home and play games. His approach goes back to the Middle Eastern culture.

During this time, I used to beg my mom to let me move out and live with her. She constantly told me no, worried about how my dad would feel. One day, she spoke to a friend of hers, who would end up giving me an opportunity to become much more than a kid living in his childhood bedroom.

I was 19 when Thomas Leffler gave me a chance to intern for him. It was initially supposed to be an unpaid internship, but he insisted on paying me for my time. Thomas was a very fair and ethical person. I learned a lot from him in a short amount of time. One day, Thomas's partner asked me if I knew anything about websites. He knew I wanted to get into working with software and technology. I said no, but that I could probably figure it out. I will never forget the words he said to me.

"You can try, but probably won't get it," he said.

After some time searching on Google, within a week, I learned enough to modify the website.

At that point, I was offered a full-time job. Finally, with a solid job, it was time for me to move out and live on my own. My mom helped me by cosigning my first lease, and I was able to manage my expenses myself, thanks to my new job.

These days I am the Chief Technology Officer for an RFID company. I have a great deal of responsibility and love what I do! I oversee operations, support team implementations, and manage client relations. Additionally, I outline and design workflow processes to maximize efficiency. I was able to make a big turnaround in life, and work towards not only landing an incredible job, but being a success as an adult. I had many priceless lessons during my journey, and am thankful that I had my mom and Thomas guiding me.

UNSTOPPABLE

Chapter 10 - Each Path Can Be Different

Special Needs can be a label applied to many completely different special children. Here are stories of different special children with very different special needs and successful outcomes in very different ways.

Some Needs Were Imposed after Birth

Lois Lee, Founder of Children of The Night, works with children who have been sex trafficked. As some of you may know, she has rescued more than 11,000 children from pimps. Some of the children she works with have learning disabilities and have trouble passing the high school equivalency. We connected and started doing the advocacy and the IEPs with public school systems. We had a lot of success getting these children the kind of resources they needed in order to be somebody and to not be dependent upon prostitution. Here is Lois' story.

It seems as if there is a major misconception that they did this voluntarily, rather than entering into prostitution as a means of surviving, an outgrowth of being sexually abused often at home or early childhood sexual abuse, regardless, that readied them for prostitution. At one high school, the staff looked down on a girl because they knew her background. She was very young. I was there to advocate for the girl. We had to stop the IEP meeting at one point because she was starting to cry. The team was automatically judging her because of her background. They didn't even look at her for the child that she was.

I stopped the meeting, and I said, "If she was your daughter, would you treat her the same way you're treating her right now?" They all stopped. They said they would not. And then she cried, and we comforted her. We started the meeting again. And it was the first time that I realized how difficult it is for these children to have to rehab and get back into the system after what they've been through. They're being judged without even knowing who they are inside, what they want, what they've gone through, and where they want to go.

As with any group if of children, you have a myriad of conditions that require additional resources from the schools. You might have a child who is schizophrenic and the social worker is not going to sign papers for the psychotropic meds. Social workers have to approve any outings.

Lois commented, "You really helped our children gain access to education that otherwise wouldn't be available to them. They're entitled to it. They don't have anyone to get it for them. Under the best circumstances, most parents are at a loss at trying to access those complicated services on behalf of their children. Children without an advocate get lost in the public school system."

Every Case is Not Cognitive

I interviewed Sylvia Farbstein about her experience with her son, Brandon. Brandon was diagnosed with a rare form of dwarfism called metatropic dysplasia when he was two and a half years old. So, he had a 504, but never an IEP. His needs were all physical, which definitely presented some challenges and some friction from the school system over the years.

Very quickly, my husband and I realized that there was no source to turn to for a roadmap or answers. We had to become comfortable with the unknown. Our journey into the unknown came quickly. Brandon's growth was so much slower and his legs grew in such a way that he required two significant surgeries called bilateral osteotomies. While those were challenging times, I feel like they prepared us to go into the education system because we learned from insurance companies that people do not see things through the lens of Brandon. They're going to look for the simplest solutions, the most cost-effective solutions, but those aren't always the solutions that enable our children to be on par with their classmates. It was like a science experiment where you had to change the variables and the things that you included in your different experiments. We stumbled upon solutions as we went along.

After a while, we learned that we could request the services of an occupational therapist who could effectively evaluate a child and assess their needs. They could help you determine the best solutions so that they are able to maneuver through the classroom, hopefully, as easily as their classmates can. We followed the steps to get a 504 plan. We would have annual meetings, which is a legal requirement. I don't believe that every single teacher necessarily took the time to read the details that were in the plan. There were times that I would need to step in and make sure that he had what he needed. So many things were trial and error.

In elementary school, it was simple because he basically needed some step stools. I loved the fact that we had the occupational therapist. There wasn't just an off-the-shelf step stool. It was, "Let us build him a block so he could rest his feet when he is sitting at a classroom desk." If you think about it, for those who are shorter in stature, their feet are dangling at a normal-sized desk, which is really not optimal for circulation. They would make sure that there were step stools at the water fountains and to reach the sink in the restroom. We had to think about fire drills and all kinds of scenarios that were outside the scope of a school day.

In middle school, I had to push a little more. We thought a wheeled backpack to bring his textbooks back and forth would work. We quickly realized he was not able to lift that backpack onto the steps of a school bus. We requested that he have two sets of textbooks - one that he would keep in school and the other that he would be keep at home. When it came to Physical Education, at first, they suggested that he sit out when he's not able to do activities. After a while, we were able to arrange things like separate projects that he could do in the library. Hanging out in the school library is when he met Mrs. Ellis, the school librarian who became his confidant. To this day, they have a remarkable relationship. She believed in him every step of the way. It's important for us to realize, as parents, that educators are sometimes going to be on our team and aligned with the goals that we see for our kids.

A lot of these solutions came from out of the box thinking. I think that some school systems don't want to think outside of the box. It feels like they're giving one family a set of privileges and they might be obligated to do that for every other family. If you are in a position to have a 504 for your child, push the school systems to create innovative solutions and not be limited to the way it's always been. As a parent, you will find yourself in battles that are a no-win situation but don't let it discourage you from being ready to battle for the next thing because what I've learned is if you don't ask, you don't get.

Brandon experienced extreme bullying and ridicule in high school. After years of seeing me advocate for him, he learned to advocate for himself. With the help of a Counselor, he was able to finish high school at a junior college. He realized that his self-worth is not dependent on what other people say or do. At the age of 15, he gave a TED Talk to 1600 people live. That was the day that he discovered his passion and purpose in connecting with strangers by sharing his story and his perspective, enabling people to see themselves in how he shared himself.

He continued through his freshman year at the junior college. His speaking career was taking off at that point. At the end of the semester, he came to us and said, "I'm learning much more being out there in the real world than I am sitting in a classroom. I would like to leave school." While my husband and I believe in higher education (we both went to great universities) we also realized that it's not our life.

Brandon is 22 now. Determined advocacy on his behalf showed him how to advocate for himself, how to take charge of his life. He has never looked back with one ounce of regret. He gets hired by Fortune 500 companies to teach their professionals all kinds of skills, including living life on your own terms and not being defined by your limitations. Brandon lives independently across the country. He loves living on his own. He's out in nature, he walks on the beach. He surrounds himself with people who are friendly and happy.

We just came back from the National Speakers Association annual conference, which we attended for the first time when he was 17 years old. This year, they invited him to be one of their main stage presenters. It's a huge honor for someone his age who has only been professionally speaking for a handful of years. He has written two books. He started writing *Ten Feet Tall* when he was 18 years old. *A Kids' Book About Self-Love* is his children's book that just came out a few months ago. That is a book about celebrating your uniqueness as your superpower.

When I say Brandon became a professional speaker, it wasn't his journey alone. I had to help him launch this business. I had to reinvent myself. I negotiate his contracts and do things that I knew nothing about a handful of years ago. I feel like we, especially as mothers, need to realize how far we've come while we've helped our kids navigate through this life. We both grew beyond the adversity.

From Frustration to Behavior Problems and Beyond

Cynthia's daughter, Dorothy, was starting to struggle with reading in first grade. She was able to read the beginning words. Once things became slightly more complicated, her comprehension plummeted. A Teacher's Aide, whose daughter had a learning disability, notice that Dorothy was beginning to struggle and to withdraw from the class. She came to me and said, "I don't have the qualifications to assess your daughter, but I want you to know she really is slipping and, when she starts to read, she picks at her fingers terribly, or twists her hair." Then, we noticed that there was one ringlet that was almost becoming a dreadlock from her nervousness. We were referred to an eye doctor who provided vision therapy and we saw a lot of progress, a lot of improvement.

In the second grade, Dorothy would spell words, when copying them from side of the paper to the other side of the paper, as many as five different ways. She didn't understand how letters worked. We thought she couldn't see it. We added private tutoring with a woman who had a linguistics background to her vision therapy and we saw great improvement. However, because I have a brother with special needs, I didn't want to just put a band-aid on it. I wanted to know what the problem was. Being the curious mother that I am, I kept pushing and questioning and asking for more and more information.

Cal State Northridge has a special education department that includes an educational psychology division. Dorothy was fully assessed at the age of seven. Her assessment came back that she was performing some visual tasks at 18 months. She was seven years old, and she was reporting about 18 months on numerous skills, maybe two, two and a half years on average, with a few peaks at about five. You can imagine as a mother, with a brother who has special needs, I hit the panic button. Then I said, "I'm not going to panic, we're going to work at it."

The specialist said, "She's exceptionally intelligent. Her vocabulary's phenomenal. Her ability to understand concepts is at the top of the scores. However, you put a pencil in her hand, or some letters in front of her and she gets completely confused, loses track of whatever she was doing, or starts to withdraw, starts to act shy, and starts to really change her behavior." The assessment came down to the point where I knew she would have to repeat second grade.

We were in a private faith-based school that did not follow any recommendations or requirements. We had her fully assessed by the public School District. They concurred with Cal state Northridge that there was definitely some kind of deficit. They did not identify a particular learning disability, but what they explained was she had eye teaming issues and visual processing issues, where her eyes did not focus on the same thing at the same time. The muscles needed further development. The vision therapy continued to work on the developmental process of the anatomy. With tutoring and training we worked on things like letter comprehension and sounds. We took her out of private school and put her into second grade for the second time.

She was now in public school. She had an IEP. However, she did not qualify for special education. We were very thankful at the moment for that, because I have a brother with multiple special needs so I thought that was good. Actually, what it meant was she was in a very gray area. She wasn't sliding completely down. According to most of the tests, she was only one grade level behind, even though the fact was that she was getting maybe 30% on spelling tests, her reading proficiency was declining, her confidence was declining, her whole behavior had changed.

That assessment placed her in general education with a reading specialist. Her reading specialist saw her two or three times a week. I pushed for independent time and group reading time, because if she became embarrassed, she would withdraw even more. If she was just with an adult, she was a big pleaser, so she would try her best. If a peer was next to her, she would either revert into complete quiet, or just being a little silly. We continued with vision therapy and private tutoring. The teacher was highly qualified and worked really hard with Dorothy. By the fourth grade, the spelling still hadn't improved. She was still struggling in many areas and now dyslexia was the diagnosis. We use special paper, graph paper, to write her math problems on, and for all of her printing so she is able to see things more clearly.

This process of improving, and then flattening, and then bottoming out kept occurring every three to four years until she was a freshman in high school, and that's where we met you, Raja. We had this child who we knew was smart, but we knew she was dyslexic. She was beginning to go through one of these cycles of withdrawing, changing her behavior and becoming a little bit of a teenage brat. That doesn't sound nice but if we asked her questions, she became a little bit aggressive. She withdrew and went into her room, things like that.

You interviewed Dorothy without me and had some time to get to know her. Then we had her fully assessed by one of the doctors you recommended. That doctor was able to actually parse out the specific deficit that Dorothy has. She tested her on a lot of general educational type of things. Dorothy's considered exceptional. She has dyslexia, a minor case, with high intelligence. That high intelligence is what would come across in spoken form, but in written form she still hesitated. For example, she wanted to write that America was beautiful. She couldn't spell America and she couldn't spell beautiful. So, she wrote the USA is nice. It was the same idea, but simplified and the spelling was avoided because of her fear of failure.

After you worked with the school, Raja, she transferred to a 504 plan. The 504 plan allowed her to stay in the advanced classes that she wanted to take so that she could go to college. She was able to achieve high success by having accommodations such as separate testing placement. She didn't have to worry about kids finishing the papers before she did, getting up and distracting her.

When she was able to concentrate and have these minor accommodations, her grades soared. Dorothy proceeded to take many advanced classes. She not only took the advanced classes; she excelled in them. She graduated as valedictorian. She began to advocate for others with special needs by participating in a rally at the school district talking about special education.

She was completely changed, from being afraid of not being able to spell well, to being able to say, it doesn't matter how I spell, it's how I think that matters, and those are words that you brought out in her. Dorothy's success continues to this day. She's in college with almost straight As. I'm not the mom who says she has to get straight As. She wants it. She knows she can do it. She is driven to succeed. This is an amazing thing, considering that, early on, we were told she might never learn to read.

Without you, and without your knowledge of the Special Education system, and that particular assessment necessary for a child with dyslexia or a vision processing issue. Dorothy would not be the success she is today. I can say for a fact you pulled her out of her own emotional turmoil by seeing the intelligence that was hidden behind a spelling deficit.

She doesn't think it's a disability, she thinks it's a challenge, and challenges can be overcome, and challenges are motivating.

I think the message to the parents is twofold. If you do it for them, they cannot do it for themselves. Don't do things for your child, do it with them. And an accommodation or modification is something for the child that you do with the child, not for them, because if you take that opportunity of completing a task from a person, they'll never learn to do that task, and they won't have the confidence of having that skill. Those accommodations that you fought for, that you knew to fight for, made all the difference in her life, not just in her grades, because grades don't matter once you're out of school. It's her life, and that came from you, Raja.

Act Before Your Child Is Labeled a Problem

Behavioral problems almost always follow frustration. Often, the behavior gets more attention from a school district than the underlying causes do. Once a child gets that label, it follows throughout their school years. That was the case with Nadine Hamoui's daughter, Jenna. Here is her story from her mother's point of view.

Jenna is a special case. She's incredible, Before I got you, I felt like I was being ... I don't want to say jerked around, but I wasn't being taken seriously until you got on the phone. You started guiding me on things that they weren't providing for me, that they should have known about, like the behavioral assessment. She has a lot more behavioral issues than she does learning disability.

She has ADHD and behavioral issues. They were accommodating her ADHD more than they were her behavioral issues. I need to jump through so many hoops right now to this day. She started in kindergarten, and to this day I still can't seem to find a behavioral therapist or somebody through the school to be able to give her that help that she needs from that aspect.

She's in fifth grade, now. Because of her behavioral issues, they had to take some sort of precaution measurement. They wanted to suspend her but they said, because she's on an IEP, they have to address it differently. Two months ago, I was called in by the dean and the teacher and her learning center teacher. And I think the nurse was there. They said that moving forward, and they gave her a five-step program. The first time she's going to get, I think, sent outside the classroom. And then the second time she's going to get sent to the principal's office to spend the rest of the day there, so in-house suspension. The third step would be to spend time at home, suspended at home. And then they said before they expel her, they're going to look into giving her another assessment.

If I had not talked to you, I would not have known that they need to start with a behavioral assessment by a board-certified behavioral analyst. She's never had that and I've asked for it in every single meeting we've had.

Now, I know that I can ask for it in writing and they have to give me a plan within 15 days of the day I submit that email to them. And they have to give me a plan and, after I sign it, she gets assessed.

There's no clear guidance on how the behavioral assessment is actually done. I ask for it and then they give me an IEP plan.

They act compassionate. At the same time, the level of service feels superficial. They give her headphones to block out the noise so she can be less distracted. One of the learning center teachers actually made a very personal connection with her. That teacher was able to talk through the emotional issues Jenna was having at school. I even asked last year, "Can she go to the counselor maybe and talk to somebody when she's having one of those days?" And they said, "It's not provided like that in elementary school, that's more high school style." Thanks to you, I know that the law requires that she should easily get a counselor to talk to her once or twice a week, 15, 20 minutes, half hour, whatever the need is. Knowing that I can have your help to talk to the school is a tremendous relief.

Get Help as Early as You Can

Mark Nelson's path was more difficult because his family did not know help was available until he was in high school. Here is his story from his point of view.

Before I met you, I definitely was struggling in high school with my reading and my writing in terms of being to grade level and par. For my writing, I was around from 150 to 200 words. I definitely had a hard time composing sentences and structures. I didn't have the tools to help me at that point in terms of using computers. They were having me write a lot by hand, which definitely made it a lot harder for me to be able to express myself and get my point of view across. Anything with writing or reading was a struggle for me.

I was at a point where I was always frustrated because I'd need help. I never felt like I got adequate help. The level of curriculum was always dumbed down and not challenging me or pushing me to go farther. I did have some audio books, but many of my books were not audio. That was something that changed after I met you. I got audio books. I had a computer and tools that could help me and move me along.

It was weird to be in a state where I never felt like I was actually progressing in terms of my reading or my writing. That definitely was an area of frustration. I was doing great in all my classes, but I was never challenged to the point where I learned and progressed.

I was a sophomore when I met you. I was still having a hard time in my IEPs in terms of getting help. Mrs. Amano recommended that we get in touch with you. We didn't know that it was not normal for a School Superintendent to attend IEP meetings. With him, it was always very much hitting a wall if we wanted to try to do something or ask for help or ask for accommodations or resources; he would shut it all down. The principal of Monrovia High School said, "Hey, let's get him a computer and let's get him resources that would actually help him." That got shut down real quick by the Superintendent.

You got us an Attorney who knew how the system is supposed to work. It was scary to have that much money over our heads. I was fighting for my education, fighting for my rights. I was fighting to give myself a future. If I didn't fight for that, and just stayed where it was comfortable and where I was just given all A's, and where I didn't get the tools to succeed later in life, it would've absolutely set me up for failure. I wouldn't have been able to really compete and go on to what I did at Citrus College and being able to get my a AA and finish out those degrees.

For me, the system started to break down in elementary school when they saw that I had learning disabilities. High school is really where it broke down to the point where I knew I wasn't going to be able to reach my goals. I realized that I had a choice to have it easy or to do the harder thing and try to progress and get better. In high school, every single class I had besides my elective was an RSP SDC class that was an easier grade and set up to be that way. I knew I wasn't getting to where I needed to be.

Resources in starting them early enough to the point where they were ingrained that I saw it as a tool to help me and having it there. Because for me, the computer is such a big thing in terms of being able to listen to things. And being able to dictate things through the computer is still a big part of even what I do to this day. And if I had that tool earlier, I could only imagine how much more it would've changed. I needed resources and tools to help me adapt to my weaknesses.

If I could go back and change one thing, it would be getting resources and tools sooner. The sooner you get those tools, the sooner you can adapt to the information you're trying to read and learn. And that's the thing, a computer helped break down the material. Being able to have my books on my computer was a really big thing. I still even continued having that into when I moved on into college.

I would still say reading is difficult for me. Even to this day, with books I'm reading, I prefer to have an audio portion to go along with it. I've gotten better to the point where I don't necessarily have to heavily rely on the computer for tracking. I've gotten better at tracking myself, but audiobooks are still a huge thing that I use when I have to learn. Getting the help I needed, even if it was late in my school years, allowed me to achieve the goals I was afraid would be prevented. I got my AA at Citrus College and I finished that out with, I believe, a 3.4 GPA.

It was a big step forward to be able to complete that and finish that. When I was going to Citrus, I was doing part-time work with REI. When I graduated, I was able to shift over to being full-time at REI. I'm in charge of helping keep things organized. I also help people in terms of getting their camping gear and going out on experiences and having fun that way. Success is being able to finish out Citrus, then transition from Citrus to full-time employment. That was definitely something that was nice.

You can't let your disabilities define who you are. You can't let them always just put you back. At the end of the day, you can have tools and resources that help you go farther. In your core, you need to know that you want to move past your disabilities and try to get better. You're your own advocate. And if you can't be your own advocate, you're not going to get the help, the tools and the resources you need. You can't let your disabilities beat you down.

When Differences Are Visible

Cody Potochan was bullied in school because he is different. He has been diagnosed with Tourette syndrome, anxiety, walks on his tip toes, and has obsessive compulsive disorder. He used to get beat up by his peers. He changed high schools four times. Cody had a difficult time during school and ended up being homeschooled because the bullying was so bad. The school did not do anything to alleviate the bullying. Cody suffered much in school.

Dave, (Cody's dad) reached out to Raja because he needed help with the school. Raja was able to get him an Individual Education Plan (IEP). Dave stated that he did not think the teachers cared about Cody. He believed budgeting was more important than providing services for his son. Dave stated the teachers should be better educated with IEPs and that the IEP team is comprised of one or two parents and the majority of the team is district personnel.

Raja had Cody evaluated when he was 9. He was again evaluated, thanks to Raja, after his twin sister, Summer, died at age 18. He went through a dark period associating with the wrong crowd. He was grieving in his own way, but needed a lot of support. After his sister's death Dave asked Raja for help. Cody is maturing at his own pace and has come a long way.

Cody started building cars at around age 15. His first build, which he still owns, was a '94 Accord that he enhanced with a turbo and other high-performance parts. The second car he built was a '76 Firebird which he still owns. The baddest car he built from the wiring, the welding, and custom building was a '67 Camaro. Unfortunately, he sold it to make money.

Today Cody is 21 years old and works at an auto mechanic shop. He has been there for three consecutive years. This is a huge improvement because a few years ago Cody could not hold a job for one month. Cody works seven days a week. He advertises and works out of my garage on his off time. He gets so many calls that he has to turn work down. Dave is extremely proud of Cody and tells him that all the time.

When I asked Dave what he wants the reader to walk away with, he stated "Do not hinder your children. Allow them to make mistakes and be there for them to pick them up when they fall."

A Different Path

My name is Gerad Hopkins and I have a traumatic brain injury (TBI). School was really hard for me. Teachers didn't give me the education that I needed. They didn't help get me into a special education program. I really thought I never would like to go to school because of my public-school experience. My mom tried homeschooling me but did not see any change. She had to really try hard to be a teacher at home for me. Eventually I made some kind of educational progress.

In public school I didn't feel like myself. I was very depressed, very stressed out and afraid of everything. I got bullied. Even when my parents went to the school to report it, teachers didn't seem to have time to help.

Then, we found Raja Marhaba, which is who got me into Frostig. It's a special education school. They have smaller class sizes, and I got the attention that I didn't get in the public school.

At Frostig, they saw where I was struggling. They were able to find a way to make it easy and to explain how to do the homework. I had several teachers who would check on me to see how I was dealing with the classwork that I had trouble with. They gave me a lot of time to figure it out before I answered their questions. I had one-on-one sessions after class as well. That felt pretty good. I definitely needed more time. They offered that and I am glad I had that opportunity.

Frostig changed everything, my comprehension, my math skills, the people who I was hanging around with. I was able to have a connection with the teachers, which I never thought I would have in school. Teachers and students treated me like I was somebody. I felt like I was in a safe place. I was feeling like myself. I really enjoyed it.

My mom was able to get a guitar for me from a friend. I think what turned me on to playing the guitar was the music I was listening to. My guitar teacher was a great teacher. He was my guitar teacher for about five years. In high school, I joined an ensemble group and I did a talent show. Right after that, I felt like this is who I want to be. I turned into a person I never thought I could be by learning music. After I graduated from Frostig, I went to college. I was a music major. I'm a guitar player, I write and sing. I've been playing for almost 15 years and I'm very proud of it.

Thank you to my family for always being there and for giving me the opportunities that I never thought that I would have. Thank you to Raja for taking this process over with my family and especially staying truthful, loving, and supportive to get their son a better life and education. I also want to thank God for giving me a life that I never thought I would live. God knew this plan was coming and he brought Raja to my family because he loves all of us and he's very protective over my family, me, and Raja. Thank you to all of you for helping me and encouraging me through the years. I look forward to achieving my goals in my life every step of the way!

If I have a message for others who struggle, it's to keep going with your goals and discover what you're really searching for. When there are a lot of obstacles, find a way to push through them like I did. Sometimes it will take a while for that to happen. You'll realize you've come a long way and you'll appreciate that. I want the reader to say, "Yeah, I know what he's saying and I'm going to achieve it. I can follow the steps along the way, even though it gets hard, once I find my goal."

Never Give Up!

I hope this book will provide strength and inspiration to those who read it. Never give up on your faith or yourself no matter what. Click the links below to discover resources and find out how you too can make a difference in a child's life.

- Please visit The Jonathan Foundation website
  http://thejonathanfoundation.org/
- Like our Facebook page
  https://www.facebook.com/TheJonathanFoundation/notificati
  ons/
- Follow us on Instagram:
  https://www.instagram.com/thejonathanfoundation/

We are here for you! Your support is greatly appreciated. Help us pay it forward by saving one child at a time! Allow The Jonathan Foundation to be the wind beneath your children's wings and elevate them.

UNSTOPPABLE

Conclusion

Sometimes, we are blinded to the truth because we are too busy fighting for our own survival, and unfortunately, the people we are trying to protect get hurt the most.

Jonathan Amir Marhaba (my Pochee), I love you beyond measure

Omar Jamal Marhaba (my Jamooolttee), I love you to infinity and beyond.

This was a very difficult book to write, especially after reading my sons' true feelings decades later. I hadn't known a lot of what they disclosed until I asked them to provide me with their stories and asked them to co-write with me. It seems like a mother's tears for her children never end.

Embarking on the special education journey is not a simple task. The purpose of sharing my story and providing resources is because I do not want any family to suffer the extreme financial and emotional burdens we endured. Nor do I want marriages dissolved because of the stress. When I was going through my journey, I was married, working with my husband in the construction business, gathering evidence for attorneys, trying to understand both my sons and their challenges, constantly communicating with the schools, taking the boys for therapy, and the list goes on.

In the beginning, as a married couple, my husband and I did what we could to help our children. Little did we know about all the politics and economics. That, in and of itself, placed an even larger burden on our marriage. My husband and I are human and we can bend so much before we break. Each partner in a marriage has his/her own responsibilities and level of endurance. A special education child is an unexpected blessing that did not come with a guidebook on how to deal with the situation at hand. We both love our children unconditionally and, therefore, we will do everything and anything within our abilities to help them.

When we overextended ourselves to help our children, we failed to nourish the marriage. Where do we find the time for us when the rest of our life is in disarray? Learn from me, not from my mistakes. I do not want another child to be sacrificed for a Free and Appropriate Public Education. Our tax dollars pay for our children's public education and our children should be the beneficiaries. Unfortunately, politics, budgets and untrained district staff provide many obstacles. It can be a battle for parents to obtain the appropriate services and placements their children need in order to access grade level curriculum and progress in the school environment. Our government needs to take a closer look at the national broken special education system and ACT! Too many lives are sacrificed and lost when those same lives could have been saved.

Once a parent learns that his/her child has a challenge impeding them from progressing in school, that parent does not always know or understand how to navigate the national broken special education system. I hope this book will be a valuable resource for parents to learn from my story and to reach out for help if they feel trapped in the system. As a parent, I spent many nights crying my heart out for both my boys, not knowing which way to turn, or who to ask for help. Mind you, my journey commenced 25 years ago when I did not have Google to help me or a mentor to guide me.

This book is intended to be a hands-on book that a parent can refer to when they need help. The sad part is that 25 years later the system is still broken. I have advocated for hundreds of families and my fight for the children today is not much different from when I was fighting for my own two boys. Every day a child will be born with some sort of a challenge and parents will continue to search for help, hope, insight, and support.

The best advice I can share as a parent who has already walked the path you are currently walking, experienced horrific abuse by the system, sacrificed almost everything I had to fight for both of my sons, is to keep your eye on the prize. The prize being your children. I was consumed with guilt, pain, hurt, hopelessness, and felt alone during the entire process. With all these emotions it is easy to lose focus.

Culture plays a big role with special education families. Many times, one of the spouses is in denial or does not want to believe there is something wrong with their child. I faced this situation within my own marriage, and I believe it added to the stress and hardship I endured. It took a long time for me to persuade my husband, my side of the family and my in-laws that all the assessments, doctor appointments, IEPs, and therapies were necessary. At one point, they thought I was the one making my sons sick and there is nothing wrong with them. I am Middle Eastern, and I understand the Middle Eastern family component where men are the decision makers. Although we live in a more modernized world than years back, the culture has not changed. It becomes very challenging for a Middle Eastern couple to survive the broken special education system with those barriers. All that I ask is for stakeholders to please keep an open mind and work together in the best interest of the child. It could make the difference between keeping the family unit united or divided.

I felt guilt because I bore both these boys. At first, I did not realize that they truly are Gods' gift to me. I felt that I was the one that inflicted all their suffering upon them because I gave birth to them. They were born with deficits and they had tremendous challenges growing up in school. I felt pain because I suffered with them all those years. I was hurt because I was extremely upset with the system and how political run it is. I felt hopeless because I was losing my marriage, the business was suffering, my sons were on hold with no services, and bills were piling up. We lived in a very dark place throughout both sons elementary, middle and high school years. I felt alone, because there was nobody there to turn to, hand hold me, believe in me, understand my cry for my sons, show me the way, and let me know "it is going to be ok". I was broken!

My prayer is that this book will not only be like a "living document" where it may become a parents' reference book. I want parents not to blame themselves for giving birth to a child with special needs, as I did. This book offers resources, contact information, and hope for parents to have someone holding their hands showing them the way, letting them know they are not alone.

UNSTOPPABLE

Resources

The author does not endorse these resources, but provides the reader with information to be better informed

RESOURCE   **DESCRIPTION**

1812ada, Inc   **"Getting Ready for College and Life"** helps students assess their current thinking and practices to see what is successful and what is not. The course includes animated sections and video content integrated into a single digital platform. This innovative online course, developed by 1812ada, Inc., follows a proven syllabus from Beacon College that is delivered in a multi-modal, multi-sensory format with the digital version of Skip Downing's book, "On Course. Getting Ready for College and Life" has been provided as a 15-week semester course and an 8-week summer course. It has flexibility."
https://www.1812ada.org/

AbilityFirst   AbilityFirst strengthens and cultivates skills that give our participants the tools to successfully navigate each transition in life, including building social connections and independence; employment preparation, training and experience; and, fun and engaging activities that offer families an opportunity to refresh and recharge.
https://www.abilityfirst.org/

ADA	American Disabilities Act, U.S. Department of Justice, Civil Rights Division -Information and Technical Assistance http://www.ada.gov/
Affordable Colleges	We've created a list of the current disability scholarships offered by various foundations and organizations including a list of general scholarships for students with disabilities, as well as those specifically aimed towards students with learning disabilities, hearing or visual impairments, psychological disabilities, or mobility impairments. College resources for students with disabilities https://www.affordablecolleges.com/resources/scholarships-students-with-disabilities/ Scholarships and Financial Aid https://www.affordablecolleges.com/resources/scholarships/
Amen Clinics	Amen Clinics, Inc. is one of the world leaders in applying brain imaging science to help people who struggle with: • Emotional issues such as anxiety, depression, and bipolar disorder. • Behavioral challenges like addictions, weight control, or anger-management issues. • Cognitive problems such as memory issues, Alzheimer's Disease, and dementia. • Learning challenges like Attention Deficit Disorder (ADD), also called Attention Deficit Hyperactivity Disorder (ADHD). http://www.amenclinics.com/
American Printing House, APH Family Connect	FamilyConnect is a service offered by the American Printing House for the Blind (APH) to give parents and other family members of children who are visually impaired–and professionals who work with them–a supportive place for sharing and finding resources on raising their children from birth to

adulthood. Every parent wonders, "Will I do a good job raising my child?" If your child is blind or visually impaired, you'll have the same question…and many more. FamilyConnect has the answers. Whether your child was recently diagnosed, has been living with a visual impairment for years, or is multiply disabled, you'll find the personal support, information, and resources you need to raise a child with vision loss.

https://familyconnect.org/

American Speech and Language Hearing Association	**Speech** is how we say sounds and words. People with speech problems may: • not say sounds clearly • have a hoarse or raspy voice • repeat sounds or pause when speaking, called stuttering **Language** is the words we use to share ideas and get what we want. A person with a language disorder may have problems: • understanding • talking • reading • writing https://www.asha.org/public/speech/disorders/
American Speech and Language Hearing Association Screenings	**School-age hearing screenings are an integral** tool in identifying children with hearing loss who were not identified at birth, lost to follow-up, or who developed hearing loss later. Without mandated routine hearing screenings in schools, students with unilateral, less severe or late onset hearing loss may not be identified or will be misdiagnosed and managed. Efforts to provide consistent protocols, screener training and follow-up through school-age will help ensure that children with hearing loss are identified and managed in a timely manner, and thereby minimize negative academic consequences.

https://www.asha.org/advocacy/state/school-age-hearing-screening/

Apraxia of Speech	Apraxia of speech (AOS)—also known as acquired apraxia of speech, verbal apraxia, or childhood apraxia of speech (CAS) when diagnosed in children—is a speech sound disorder. Someone with AOS has trouble saying what he or she wants to say correctly and consistently. AOS is a neurological disorder that affects the brain pathways involved in planning the sequence of movements involved in producing speech. The brain knows what it wants to say, but cannot properly plan and sequence the required speech sound movements. https://www.nidcd.nih.gov/health/apraxia-speech
Attitude	Living Well with Attention Deficit – Resources and Information on ADD/ADHD http://www.addidtudemag.com/
Auticon	Employment for Individuals with Autism. People with autism are an asset to any team. Special talents in logic, detail and pattern recognition are typical for many people with autism as well as enormous concentration and a pronounced interest in IT, physics, mathematics and technology. People on the autism spectrum can thus make a significant contribution to outstanding performance quality in the areas of IT and compliance: Many small and medium-sized enterprises already rely on auticon for IT projects, especially in the areas of: https://auticon.us/projects-services/
Burbank Optometric Center	Equipped to care for all of your vision needs at any age. Examine infants as young as six months of age through the InfantSee program. At Burbank Optometric Center, Inc., our optometry staff works together to ensure your visit is comfortable and completed in a timely manner. We

have a qualified team of professionals that will work around your busy schedule and address any questions or concerns prior to the appointment. Whether it's a general eye exam or treating a condition that requires an in depth diagnosis, our team provides undivided attention to each patient so we can evaluate a plan based on your needs and our professional opinion. Our doctor offers full vision examinations and will diagnose and treat an array of eye diseases and conditions to keep your eyes healthy!
http://www.burbankvision.com/

Center for Healing the Human Spirit	Psychotherapy, Neuro-Linguistic Psychology and Hypnotherapy, Building Strengths and Resolving Weaknesses, Depression and Anxiety, Communication, Compulsions and Addictions, Body Awareness and Body Image, Health and Well-Being, ADHD Psychotherapy, ADHD Coaching, Strategies for Learning and Attentional Challenges, ADDventures in Achievement http://www.healingthehumanspirit.com/.
Cerebral-Palsy	Cerebral palsy is a result of brain damage or abnormal brain development that affects an individual's ability to control their muscles. It is most likely to develop within the first month following a child's birth, or even during the first years of their life when their brain is still developing. Doctors and scientists used to believe that cerebral palsy was predominantly a result of oxygen deprivation during birth. However, recent research suggests that this actually accounts for a small number of cases. Congenital cerebral palsy, which is caused by abnormal brain development or damage occurring before or during birth, accounts for the majority (85%-90%) of all cases. https://birthinjurycenter.org/cerebral-palsy/

CHADD	AN OVERVIEW GUIDE OF ADHD Everybody can have difficulty sitting still, paying attention or controlling impulsive behavior once in a while. For some people, however, the problems are so pervasive and persistent that they interfere with every aspect of their life: home, academic, social and work. Attention-deficit/hyperactivity disorder (ADHD) is a neurodevelopmental disorder affecting 11 percent of school-age children. Symptoms continue into adulthood in more than three-quarters of cases. ADHD is characterized by developmentally inappropriate levels of inattention, impulsivity and hyperactivity. www.chadd.org
Department of Rehabilitation	The Department of Rehabilitation (DOR) Assists individuals with disabilities to build viable careers and live independently in their community. DOR's Vocational Rehabilitation Program provides a variety of services including career guidance and counseling, job search and interview skills training, independent living skills, on the job training, employment preparation, assistive technology, and other services. There is a DOR in every state. Google Department of Rehabilitation/Vocational Rehabilitation. https://www.dor.ca.gov/
Disability Specific Scholarships	How will you pay for college, what career should you pursue, and how can you access the best college resources? Questions like these arise before high school graduation and again when applying to graduate programs. Navigating the college application process might feel overwhelming at times, so we offer resources to help. Find support on topics including finding financial aid resources, choosing a major, and safely enjoying campus life. https://affordablecolleges.com/resources/scholarships-students-with-disabilities

Draft Builder 6	Reading and Writing Resources – Software programs to help access grade level curriculum http://www.donjohnston.com/
Due Process Hearing	Information on the path of a due process hearing https://www.parentcenterhub.org/details-dueprocess/
Easy Essay	http://www.theeasyessay.com
EduBirdie	Having disabilities is not an obstacle for students to enter a college. Various organizations work to help people with disabilities to overcome social, physical, attitudinal or other difficulties and avoid exclusion from many areas of life. Many employers nowadays offer opportunities for them to earn decent money. And there are multiple resources, software programs, and technological devices to help young people with different disabilities to obtain a proper education and subsequent benefits. https://edubirdie.com/
Exceptional Minds	Exceptional Minds is an academy and studio preparing young adults on the autism spectrum for careers in animation, visual effects, 3D gaming and other related fields in the entertainment industry. We provide technical and work readiness training customized to help students achieve their full artistic and professional potential. Exceptional Minds is comprised of a vocational academy, post graduate program, and professional post-production studios. https://exceptional-minds.org/
Federal Rights	Frequently asked questions about Section 504 and Individuals with disabilities https://www2.ed.gov/about/offices/list/ocr/504faq.html
Federal Statute	Information and links to U.S. Department of Education, Office of Special Education and

Rehabilitation Services (OSERS), Office of Special Education (OSEP), OSERS Blog, IDEA by State, Contacts, IDEA Statue of Contacts, Building the Legacy: IDEA 2004
https://sites.ed.gov/idea/statute-chapter-33

Fit Learners

Fit Learning is not a one-size, fits all tutoring center in Los Angeles. We help our learners build fluency in core academic skills by combining learning science, precision teaching, and curriculum-based assessment. The result is learners who are confident, possess the ability to expertly perform in any classroom environment, and who acquire a newfound capacity for learning.
https://fitlearners.com/centers/los-angeles-canoga-park/

Great Schools

Find A School Near You
GreatSchools is the leading nonprofit providing high-quality information that supports **parents** pursuing a great education for their child, **schools** striving for excellence, and **communities** working to diminish inequities in education.
Over 49 million users visit our award-winning website each year to learn about schools in their area, explore research insights, and access thousands of free, evidence-based parenting resources to support their child's learning and well-being.
http://www.greatschools.org/

Grizzly Youth Academy (GYA)

This is a partnership between the Calfornia National Guard and the Grizzly Challenge Charter School. This grades intervention program is for boys or girls between the ages of 15 1/2 to 18 who are struggling with their grades or participation in school. They offer a highly-structured environment that promotes leadership, cooperation, and academic skills, while also building self-

esteem, pride, and confidence. This is a voluntary
academy by application only. All who apply must commit
to finishing the 22 week on-campus phase away from
family and other influences.
www.grizzlyyouthacademy.org

Guide to Affordable Student Housing	How will you pay for college, what career should you pursue, and how can you access the best college resources? Questions like these arise before high school graduation and again when applying to graduate programs. Navigating the college application process might feel overwhelming at times, so we offer resources to help. Find support on topics including finding financial aid resources, choosing a major, and safely enjoying campus life. https://www.affordablecolleges.com/resources/colleg e-student-housing-guide
IDEA (Special Education Law)	Welcome to the U.S. Department of Education's Individuals with Disabilities Education Act (IDEA) website, which brings together IDEA information and resources from the Department and our grantees. Whether you are a student, parent, educator, service provider, or grantee, you are here because you care about children with disabilities and their families and want to find information and explore resources on infants, toddlers, children, and youth with disabilities. https://sites.ed.gov/idea/
IDEA State Contacts	Office of Special Education Programs (OSEP)/Monitoring & State Improvement Planning Division (MSIP) State Lead, IDEA Part B and Part C. Contacts. Provides contact information for a representative in each state. https://www2.ed.gov/policy/speced/guid/idea/monito r/state-contact-list.html
Inspiration Software, Inc.	Writing and Thinking Skills Simple to use, but powerful in the impact it has on users, **Inspiration 10** is the ideal visual thinking tool

for creating mind maps, concept maps, graphic organizers, outlines and presentations with ease! Our visual mapping tool makes it easy to quickly capture your ideas and visually organize them to communicate concepts and strengthen understanding. Transfer your visual diagram to a written outline in just one-click, perfect for structuring writing plans for papers and reports.
https://www.inspiration-at.com/inspiration-10/

International Society for Neuroregulation & Research	Neurofeedback and Biofeedback Watch the video explaining Neurofeedback in simple terms. Find explanations and descriptions of many aspects of Neurofeedback. What i s Neurofeedback? What is Biofeedback? These questions are answered here. These definitions were created by the ISNR for the purposes of identifying what Neurofeedback and Biofeedback are and what they are not. https://isnr.org/resources
Irlen Syndrome	What is Irlen Syndrome? Irlen Syndrome (also referred to at times as Meares-Irlen Syndrome, Scotopic Sensitivity Syndrome, and Visual Stress) is a perceptual processing disorder. It is not an optical problem. It is a problem with the brain's ability to process visual information. This problem tends to run in families and is not currently identified by other standardized educational or medical tests. The Irlen Method provides a unique service for some children and adults identified with reading and learning difficulties, low motivation, attention deficit disorder (ADHD), discipline problems, headaches and migraines, autism, and traumatic brain injury. The symptoms of Irlen Syndrome are wide-ranging, but our technology focuses on one core problem: the brain's inability to process visual information. You don't have to have a diagnosed reading or learning problem benefit from the Irlen Method. Even good readers and gifted students can be helped.

https://irlen.com/what-is-irlen-syndrome/#
https://irlen.com/who-we-help/

Kurzweil Educational Systems	Kurzweil products provide students with access to text as well as comprehensive reading, writing, study skills, research, and test taking tools. The software aligns with Common Core State Standards and is highly customizable for individual special education needs or to support inclusion in the classroom. http://www.kurzweiledu.com
LD Online	Resources at school and at home to provide the right tools for children that learn differently. http://www.ldonline.org/?ID=16
Learning Ally	There's a reason we're passionate about literacy. After all, it's the foundation of learning. Yet, today, 65% of fourth graders in the U.S. read below proficiency levels and are 400% more likely to drop out of high school. For the most vulnerable students - black, indigenous and people of color (BIPOC), low income, English Language Learners and students with learning disabilities - the crisis is even more acute, and has persisted for decades. Our educational ecosystems require a new response to the needs of our students. https://learningally.org/About-Us/Who-We-Are
Let's Talk LD	It is our mission to meet learners with special needs where they are, at critical periods in their development and learning, in an effort to implement innovative programs that can support these learners in living productive and fulfilling academic, social, and professional lives defined by self-sufficiency, self-determination, and purpose. Click HERE to learn more about Let's Talk LD. https://www.letstalkld.org/
Livescribe	Write Less and Listen More. Smartpen, Smartpaper, Livescribe+ are devices and apps. The bridge

between audio and script. Writing, recording and repeating.
http://www.livescribe.com/en-us/

Making Math Real	Making Math Real is the first and only simultaneous multisensory structured methodology in math. To prepare all educators, including parents and homeschool parents, tutors, learning specialists, and teachers to provide comprehensive, structured numeracy development to ensure students of all ages receive the highest quality math education they need and deserve. http://www.makingmathreal.org/
Math Games	Math games for children making learning fun https://www.mathschase.com/
Meet The Biz	https://meetthebiz.net/about-us/
Microsoft Autism	Hiring Program Microsoft Neurodiversity Hiring Program & FAQ We built the Microsoft Neurodiversity Hiring Program on the belief that neurodivergent individuals strengthen a workforce with innovative thinking and creative solutions. Diverse teams positively impact our company culture, working environment and how we serve our customers. The Neurodiversity Hiring program seeks to attract talented neurodivergent candidates and provide the training and support needed for career growth and success. Through this program, applicants engage in an extended interview process that focuses on workability, interview preparation, and skill assessment. Our process gives candidates the opportunity to showcase their unique talents while learning about Microsoft as an employer of choice. https://www.microsoft.com/en-us/diversity/inside-microsoft/cross-disability/neurodiversityhiring

NanoPac, Inc.   NanoPac supplies products and services for
individuals with disabilities (low vision, blindness,
reading disabilities, quadriplegia, blind, Legally
Blind, reading machines, environmental controls,
voice activation, augmentative communications,
hearing impairments, voice recognition, speech
synthesis, text to speech, switches and switch
mounts, magnifiers, and door openers).
http://www.nanopac.com

Private School   Search for schools on a national level. Just input the
Search   state and/or Zip code. If the site takes to a page that
states no results found. Look at the bottom of the
page for links to Public Schools, Public School
Districts, Public Libraries. Click any of them and a
list will appear.
https://nces.ed.gov/surveys/pss/privateschoolsearch/

RespectAbility   RespectAbility is a diverse, disability-led nonprofit
that works to create systemic change in how society
views and values people with disabilities, and that
advances policies and practices that empower people
with disabilities to have a better future. Our mission
is to fight stigmas and advance opportunities so
people with disabilities can fully participate in all
aspects of community.
https://www.respectability.org/

Rightstartmath   A Multisensory Structured Professional Development
Program to Reach the Full Diversity of Learners, K-
12
A Hands-on Approach to Mathematics
https://rightstartmath.com/

Semel   Semel Institute for Neuroscience and Human
Institute   Behavior. Welcome to the inaugural newsletter of
the Department of Psychiatry and Semel Institute at
UCLA. Our mission is to advance the mental health
and well-being of the population through cutting-

edge translational research, state-of-the-art clinical care, and training the next generation of leaders in mental health. Central to this mission is continuing to build diversity in our faculty, staff, and trainees, who manifest our commitment to health equity and inclusion.
http://www.semel.ucla.edu

SiliconValley4U	Code Yourself Real World Product We offer a wide variety of project-based coding courses, internships, and resources to empower young students with modern skills and experience. https://www.siliconvalley4u.com/
SOAR	Searchable Online Accommodations Resource JAN's Searchable Online Accommodation Resource (SOAR) system is designed to let users explore various accommodation options for people with disabilities in work and educational settings. These accommodation ideas are not all inclusive. If you do not find answers to your questions, please contact JAN directly. The staff of experienced consultants is happy to discuss specific accommodation needs in a confidential manner. https://askjan.org/soar.cfm
Special Education Rights and Responsibilities (SERR) (Google SERR for your State)	The Federal and California special education laws give eligible students with disabilities the right to receive a free appropriate public education (FAPE) in the least restrictive environment (LRE). This manual explains how to become eligible for special education, how to request and advocate for special education services, and what to do if you disagree with school districts. https://serr.disabilityrightsca.org/
The Spectrum Works	We believe that people with autism can be integrated into the workforce through education and opportunity. Our vision is to change society's

perception of how corporations can seamlessly employ and integrate people with autism into their workplace.
https://www.spectrumworks.org/

Tri-Counties Regional Center	TCRC provides person and family centered planning, services and supports for individuals with developmental disabilities to maximize opportunities and choices for living, working, learning and creating in the community. https://www.tri-counties.org/
Wrightslaw Evaluations	Individual Education Evaluations Parents and school officials are often confused about what an independent educational evaluation (IEE) is and how the evaluation should be used. This article addresses the right to an IEE, what constitutes an IEE, the value of an IEE, what the law requires of school districts, who is financially responsible for an IEE, and who can conduct an IEE. https://www.wrightslaw.com/info/test.iee.steedman.htm
Wrightslaw Legal Library	Parents, advocates, educators, and attorneys come to Wrightslaw for accurate, up-to-date information about special education law and advocacy for children with disabilities. The Caselaw Library includes a sample of decisions on special education legal issues and does not include every important decision since the law was enacted. If you are looking for Complaints filed in federal court, please check the Federal Court Complaints page. If you are looking for articles about legal issues, please check the Articles and Analyses page. For additional information about cases and legal research, please check the Directory of Legal and Advocacy Resources. For articles about special education law and advocacy topics, frequently asked questions, and newsletter archives, please go to

the Advocacy Library. The cases listed below were derived from https://www.wrightslaw.com/.

Successful Cases That Might Help You

Free and Appropriate Public Education (FAPE)

https://www.caledattorney.com/post/oah-case-no-2020100618
https://www.californiaspecialedlaw.com/wiki/hearing-decisions/2019120387/
https://casetext.com/case/jb-v-tuolumne-cnty-superintendent-of-sch-3

New in 2021

Rogich v. Clark County School District, (Nevada, 2021). Methodology and procedural safeguards case. School district failed to provide an IEP that identified an Orton-Gillingham based methodology or structured literacy format that teachers would have to use to meet the needs of a child with dyslexia; school district refused to accept the parents' offer to pay to train teachers in an effective structured literacy method; IEP teams failed to adequately review evaluations provided by parents and failed to "meaningfully consider parents' concerns for enhancing their child's education." Judge held that telling parents "Trust us to provide what she needs" is "not sufficient."

S.S. v. Cobb Co. Sch. Dist. (N.D. GA 2021) - When "a due process complaint is dismissed without an evidentiary hearing and the reviewing court lacks findings and conclusions on the merits of the plaintiff's claims . . . remand is the most appropriate remedy." Case remanded for due process hearing.

S.C. v. Lincoln Co. Sch. Dist. (9th Cir. 2021) - Administrative law judge held that school district failed to provide child with Prader-Willi Syndrome with a FAPE because child required "total food security" in a schoolwide environment to obtain a meaningful educational benefit;

ordered placement at an educational center where these needs could be met. District Court denied parent's request for "stay put". Ninth Circuit reversed denial, remanded for entry of stay-put order at the educational center at school district's expense.

Previous Cases

Fry v. Napoleon Comm. Sch. District began as a case about a school's refusal to allow a child's service dog to accompany her in school. After the parents sued for damages under Section 504 and the ADAA, a federal appeals court held that the parents' claim was barred because they failed to exhaust their administrative remedies under the IDEA.

On June 28, 2016, the U. S. Supreme Court granted certiorari in Fry v. Napoleon Comm. Sch. District. Click to learn more about the Fry case, read earlier decisions, and briefs filed with the Supreme Court. In 2017, the U.S. Supreme Court issued a unanimous decision for child and parents.

In *Endrew F. v. Douglas County School District RE-1*, the parents argued that their child with autism did not make measurable progress on his IEP goals and that the school failed to address his worsening behavior problems. The parents advocated for a heightened 'meaningful educational benefit' standard. On December 22, 2015, after an adverse decision from a federal appeals court, the parents requested that the Supreme Court resolve their educational benefit question. On September 29, 2016, the Supreme Court agreed to hear the case.

Endrew F. v. Douglas County School District RE-1 (No. 15-827) (2017), U.S. Supreme Court unanimously rejected the "de minimis" standard for one that is "markedly more demanding than the 'merely more than de minimis' test applied by the 10th Circuit." In his opinion, Chief Justice Roberts wrote, "a student offered an educational program providing 'merely more than de minimis' progress from year to year can hardly be said to have been offered an education at all."

Doug C. v. Hawaii (9th Cir. 2013) - Important decision about parental participation at IEP meetings. "All special education staff who conduct IEP meetings should be familiar with this landmark ruling about IEP meetings and parental participation" (Pete Wright)

F. H. v. Memphis City Schools (6th Cir. 2014) - Parent filed suit against school after child was verbally, physically, and sexually abused by his aides at school. School entered into Settlement Agreement with the parent, then refused to honor the Agreement. Court found that Sec. 1983 claims do not require exhaustion under IDEA and that settlement agreement is enforceable in courts.

A.C. v. Shelby County (6th Cir. 2013) - Pro-child 504 retaliation decision in which a principal filed false child abuse allegations against child's parents. For a case of this nature to proceed, there must be a finding that the school district retaliated against the parents for asserting their rights under Section 504. The Sixth Circuit's 29 page opinion does an exceptional job of explaining the basis and criteria needed for a successful Section 504 suit to proceed against a school district.

UNSTOPPABLE

About the Author

Raja B. Marhaba, Founder and CEO of The Jonathan Foundation for Children with Learning Disabilities

Ms. Marhaba has established a nonprofit organization in 2001 (The Jonathan Foundation for Children with Learning Disabilities, Inc. – www.thejonathanfoundation.org)

Raja was recognized in The San Fernando Valley Business Journal in 2002 for "Learning the Hard Way". Raja Marhaba won a Scholarship to The Anderson School of Business at UCLA - Business Development Entrepreneur Program, graduated in February 2004. She was selected and successfully completed the first cohort of the federally-funded Special Education Advocate Training (SEAT) Program in 2006. After her completion of the SEAT Program, she was selected to be a member of the Education Panel & Committee for the Juvenile Division of the Los Angeles County Superior Court, which is comprised of special education attorneys and advocates, who are court-appointed to represent the educational needs of children involved in the foster care and probation systems.

Raja Marhaba holds a certificate in Paralegal Studies with a Concentration in Litigation and Corporations from the University of California, Los Angeles, an American Bar Association Certificate Program (2009). In 2016 she received Enterprising Women of the Year Award, and her Construction Co. made the 2017 Inc. 5000 fastest growing company by industry and revenue list. She graduated the Birthing of Giants Fellowship Program, June 2018 hosted by Inc. 500.

She is the recipient for the 2019 L'Oréal Paris Women of Worth Awards, December 2019 she was recognized by the Daily News for her accomplishments with The Jonathan Foundation. December 2019 The San

Fernando Valley Business Journal recognized her for her work with The Jonathan Foundation, she has been asked by Arianna Huffington to write articles about The Jonathan Foundation and other topics that are community based for her online newspaper, Thrive Global. She was honored on the 11th Multicultural International Motion Picture Association as a 2020 Lady in Red Diamond Rose Award recipient for her work

After 25 years of working with parents to get the best available Special Education Services for an IEP or 504 Plan for their unstoppable children, Raja has recognized the career God chose for her. Learn more at https://unstoppableadvocacy.com/

Awards

- **2021 The Diane Lipton Award**
  COPAA Board Announces the 2021 Diane Lipton Award for Outstanding Advocacy Recipient Raja B. Marhaba, California, for her work to help students and families who strive for guidance and support in navigating the right path for their children. The Jonathan Foundation does just that and more. Knowledge is power, especially when it comes to disseminating information to families in such desperate need. Parents are the biggest advocates for their children. Through her foundation, Ms. Marhaba, through her own personal journey with her son, gained an incredible amount of knowledge, courage and drive to carry out this level of support by extending it to other families. Raja has touched so many families through her work and has had a profound impact in altering the course of many of these young people's lives-- many of whom, who were at risk for giving up on their hopes and dreams because they were not receiving the support and services they needed. For many years Raja has provided pro bono services to America's sex trafficking victims through Children of the Night. She is fearless in her advocacy and commands respect and action from members of the educational community who have routinely denied services to this vulnerable population.
  https://www.copaa.org/page/DianeLipton

161

- **Raja Marhaba was included in, The San Fernando Valley Business Journal Sixth annual Valley 200**
  A special standalone book featuring short profiles of the most influential leaders in the Valley area. Given her stature, and involvement in the valley from Martec Construction to The Jonathan Foundation, and her involvement with Val*Pac (San Fernando Valley Business Political Action Committee) she was honored amongst the elite in her community.
- **Raja Bishara Marhaba has been Inducted into the Prestigious Marquis Who's Who Biographical Registry**
  Prestigious Marquis Who's Who Biographical Registry honor description Prestigious Marquis Who's Who Biographical Registry issued a Press Release on Raja Marhaba's 2020 Induction
- **The Daily Point of Light Award**
  The Daily Point of Light Award is presented by @PointsofLight each day, celebrating the power of individuals to spark change and improve the world. I am honored to be today's Daily Point of Light for the work I do with The Jonathan Foundation for Children With Learning Disabilities.
- **2020 Lady in Red Diamond Rose Honoree**
  11th Multicultural International Motion Picture Association as a 2020 Lady in Red Diamond Rose Honoree for her work with The Jonathan Foundation.
- **2019 L'Oreal Paris Women of Worth Award**
  Honored for her work with The Jonathan Foundation https://www.lorealparisusa.com/women-of-worth/honorees/2019/raja-b-marhaba
- **Martec Construction, Inc. 5000 List**
  July 2017 Martec Construction, Inc. made the Inc. 5000 list for being one of the fastest private growing companies. A huge recognition.
- **2016 Enterprising Women of the Year Award**
- **2009 University of California, Los Angeles, an American Bar Association Certificate Program**
- **2004 Special Education Advocate Training (SEAT)**

Resilience and perseverance in any situation definitely pays off!!

Publications

The National Digest
https://thenationaldigest.com/taking-on-the-nations-educational-system-to-benefit-children-with-special-needs-the-jonathan-foundations-inspiring-story-raja-marhaba/

EP Magazine
https://reader.mediawiremobile.com/epmagazine/issues/207978/viewer?page=42
https://reader.mediawiremobile.com/epmagazine/issues/208213/viewer?page=29

Thrive
Ms. Marhaba has published articles for Arianna Huffington Thrive online publication
https://thriveglobal.com/authors/raja-marhaba/

Articles about Ms. Marhaba and The Jonathan Foundation

Granada Hills woman's efforts to fight for kids with learning disabilities honored
https://www.dailynews.com/2019/12/02/granada-hills-womans-efforts-to-fight-for-special-needs-kids-honored/?fbclid=IwAR1PHZKSixpkQabWq16JA-R0gXYu8QxmQJvzBzVXH7rhyw2dSC09qOfq-Xo

Nonprofit's $10,000 Grant From L'Oréal Paris Women of Worth
http://www.sfvbj.com/news/2019/dec/09/nonprofits-10000-grant-loreal/

MIMPA Celebrates 11th Annual Gala with 10 Honorees. Founder of The Jonathan Foundation, Raja Marhaba was one of the ten.
https://www.einnews.com/pr_news/503919101/mimpa-celebrates-11th-annual-gala-with-10-honorees-to-benefit-special-needs-network?fbclid=IwAR1eX1Lq9q8RYTL7ErA2NlQkMHi21Yni-O_v5kQCS9yogh0XFvzarLWqIH8

2019 L'Oréal Paris Women of Worth
10 Influential Women You Should Know
https://www.lorealparisusa.com/beauty-magazine/beauty-tips/beauty-trends/influential-women-of-worth.aspx?fbclid=IwAR2TbmjdGoJReuXiMVN-BRoLeKhfcZQYgYczbhvnhUv4AYJDr5pLgE9aRM0

Raja Marhaba 2019 L'Oréal Paris Women of Worth
https://www.lorealparisusa.com/women-of-worth/honorees/2019/raja-b-marhaba

George H.W. Bush, Founder of Points of Light
https://www.pointsoflight.org/?s=raja+marhaba

Mom Starts Foundation to Help Children with Learning Disabilities
https://www.pointsoflight.org/awards/mom-starts-foundation-to-help-children-with-learning-disabilities/

Raynbow Affair Magazine #1 LGBT Magazine On The Planet
https://raynbowaffair.com/loreal-paris-women-of-worth-recognizes-californias-raja-b-marhaba-founder-of-the-jonathan-foundation-for-children-with-learning-disabilities/

Voyage LA, Meet Raja Marhaba of The Jonathan Foundation for Children With Learning Disabilities
http://voyagela.com/interview/meet-jonathan-foundation-children-learning-disabilities-granada-hills-ca/

Social Media

https://www.facebook.com/TheJonathanFoundation/
https://www.linkedin.com/in/raja-amy-marhaba-5a985b14/
https://www.instagram.com/thejonathanfoundation/

UNSTOPPABLE

"Everyone starts at the bottom, but for me, I started underground. When I emerged, a mountain that exceeded the clouds had presented itself. No matter how long I climbed, the top was never near, but if I tried to go back, there was always someone pushing me up."

- Jonathan Amir Marhaba

UNSTOPPABLE

About Defining Moments Press

Built for aspiring authors who are looking to share transformative ideas with others throughout the world, Defining Moments Press offers life coaches, healers, business professionals, and other non-fiction or self-help authors a comprehensive solution to getting their books published without breaking the bank or taking years.

Defining Moments Press prides itself on bringing readers and authors together to find tools and solutions.

As an alternative to self-publishing or signing with a major publishing house, we offer full profits to our authors, low-priced author copies, and simple contract terms.

Most authors get stuck trying to navigate the technical end of publishing. The comprehensive publishing services offered by Defining Moments Press mean that your book will be designed by an experienced graphic artist, available in printed, hard copy format, and coded for all eBook readers, including the Kindle, iPad, Nook, and more.

We handle all of the technical aspects of your book creation so you can spend more time focusing on your business that makes a difference for other people.

Defining Moments Press founder, publisher, and #1 bestselling author Melanie Warner has over 20 years of experience as a writer, publisher, master life coach, and accomplished entrepreneur.

You can learn more about Warner's innovative approach to self-publishing or take advantage of free trainings and education at: www.MyDefiningMoments.com.

Defining Moments Book Publishing

If you're like many authors, you have wanted to write a book for a long time, maybe you have even started a book...but somehow, as hard as you have tried to make your book a priority, other things keep getting in the way.

Some authors have fears about their ability to write or whether or not anyone will value what they write or buy their book. For others, the challenge is making the time to write their book or having accountability to finish it.

It's not just finding the time and confidence to write that is an obstacle. Most authors get overwhelmed with the logistics of finding an editor, finding a support team, hiring an experienced designer, and figuring out all the technicalities of writing, publishing, marketing, and launching a book. Others have actually written a book and might have even published it but did not find a way to make it profitable.

For more information on how to participate in our next Defining Moments Author Training program, visit: www.MyDefiningMoments.com. Or you can email melanie@MyDefiningMoments.com.

Other Books By Defining Moments Press

Defining Moments: Coping With the Loss of a Child - Melanie Warner

Defining Moments SOS: Stories of Survival - Melanie Warner and Amber Torres

Write your Bestselling Book in 8 Weeks or Less and Make a Profit - Even if No One Has Ever Heard of You - Melanie Warner

Become Brilliant: Roadmap From Fear to Courage – Shiran Cohen

Unspoken: Body Language and Human Behavior For Business - Shiran Cohen

Rise, Fight, Love, Repeat: Ignite Your Morning Fire - Jeff Wickersham

Life Mapping: Decoding the Blueprint of Your Soul - Karen Loenser

Ravens and Rainbows: A Mother-Daughter Story of Grit, Courage and Love After Death – L. Grey and Vanessa Lynn

Pivot You! 6 Powerful Steps to Thriving During Uncertain Times – Suzanne R. Sibilla

A Workforce Inspired: Tools to Manage Negativity and Support a Toxic-Free Workplace – Dolores Neira

Journey of 1000 Miles: A Musher and His Huskies' Journey on the Century-Old Klondike Trails - Hank DeBruin and Tanya McCready

7 Unstoppable Starting Powers: Powerful Strategies For Unparalled Results From Your First Year as a New Leader – Olusegun Eleboda

Bouncing Back From Divorce With Vitality & Purpose: A Strategy For Dads – Nigel J Smart, PHD

Focus on Jesus and Not the Storm: God's Non-negotiables to Christians in America - Keith Kelley

Stepping Out, Moving Forward: Songs and Devotions - Jacqueline O'Neil Kelley

Time Out For Time In: How Reconnecting With Yourself Can Help You Bond With Your Child in a Busy Word - Jerry Le

The Sacred Art of Off Mat Yoga: Whisper of Wisdom Forever – Shakti Barnhill

The Beauty of Change: The Fun Way For Women to Turn Pain Into Power & Purpose – Jean Amor Ramoran

From No Time to Free Time: 6 Steps to Work/Life Balance For Business Owners - Christoph Nauer

Self-Healing For Sexual Abuse Survivors: Tired of Just Surviving, Time to Thrive - Nickie V. Smith

Prepared Bible Study Lessons: Weekly Plans For Church Leaders - John W. Warner

Frog on a Lily Pad - Michael Lehre

How to Effectively Supercharge Your Career as a CEO - Giorgio Pasqualin

Rising From Unsustainable: Replacing Automobiles and Rockets - J.P. Sweeney

Food - Life's Gift for Healing: Simple, Delicious & Life Saving Whole Food Plant Based Solutions - Angel and Terry Grier

Harmonize All of You With All: The Leap Ahead in Self-Development - Artie Vipperla

Powerless to Powerful: How to Stop Living in Fear and Start Living Your Life - Kat Spencer

Living with Dirty Glasses: How to Clean thos Dirty Glasses and Gain a Clearer Perspective Of Your Life - Leah Spelt Ligia

The Road Back to You: Finding Your Way After Losing a Child to Suicide - Trish Simonson

Gavin Gone: Turning Pain into Purpose to Create a Legacy - Rita Gladding

The Health Nexus: TMJ, Sleep Apnea, and Facial Development, Causations and Treatment - Robert Perkins DDS

Samantha Jean's Rainbow Dream: A Young Foster Girl's Adventure into the Colorful World of Fruits & Vegetables - AJ Autieri - Luciano

Please Excuse My Brave: Overcoming Fear and Living Out Your Purpose - Anisa L. Wesley

Unstoppable: A Parent's Survival Guide for Special Education Services with an IEP or 504 Plan - Raja Marhaba